THE SCHOOL of GREATNESS

A REAL-WORLD GUIDE TO LIVING BIGGER, LOVING DEEPER, AND LEAVING A LEGACY

LEWIS HOWES

RODALE.

© 2015 by Lewis Howes

Simultaneously published as trade hardcover
and international paperback by Rodale Inc.

Rodale books may be purchased for business or promotional use or for special sales. For information, please e-mail: BookMarketing@Rodale.com

Printed in the United States of America

Rodale Inc. makes every effort to use acid-free ♾, recycled paper ♻.

Book design by Joanna Williams

Library of Congress Cataloging-in-Publication Data
is on file with the publisher.

ISBN-13: 978–1–62336–596–7   trade hardcover
ISBN-13: 978–1–62336–714–5   international paperback
ISBN-13: 978–1–62336–902–6   trade paperback

Distributed to the trade by Macmillan

   4 6 8 10 9 7 5 trade hardcover
 2 4 6 8 10 9 7 5 3 international paperback
     8 10 9 7 trade paperback

We inspire and enable people to improve their lives and the world around them.
rodalebooks.com

To my family, this book is for you,
Diana, Ralph, Chris, Heidi, and Katherine.
Thank you for encouraging me to chase my dreams,
guiding me spiritually, showing me how to be
of service in the world, and teaching me grace, patience,
and most of all, love.

CONTENTS

CONTENTS

PREFACE

You were born with potential.

You were born with goodness and trust. You were born with ideals and dreams. You were born with greatness.

You were born with wings.

You are not meant for crawling, so don't.

You have wings.

Learn to use them and fly.

—Rumi

For the last few years, I've felt like the luckiest guy on earth. Every week, my job has been to study at an elite and exclusive—but entirely unofficial—university, a mythical academy where the world's greatest men and women teach, lecture, and pay forward the amazing knowledge they've accumulated on their paths to becoming the best in the world at what they do.

My professors were Olympic gold medalists, award-winning musicians, *New York Times* best-selling authors, world-changing activists and philanthropists, enormously successful entrepreneurs, and inspiring experts and thinkers. I was fortunate enough to be their student, audit their classes, and learn things from each of them

that I will carry with me forever. I consider this education
the greatest gift I've ever been given.

Deep down, all of us suspect—we *hope*—something
like this exists somewhere, but we just have no idea
where it is or how to get in. Our world is swimming in
information and data, unlike at any other point in human
history, and for years that has been intoxicating to many
of us. We could type anything into the Google search bar
and we'd have a million answers in a millionth of a second. We could pick a topic and go down the Wikipedia
rabbit hole for hours, if not days. But eventually, information for curiosity's sake wasn't enough. We needed more.
We wanted to know how to apply it to the world and to
our lives. We wanted knowledge and wisdom, not just 1s
and 0s. We think that places like the World Economic
Forum in Davos are maybe where we can find it. Or Summit Series. Or TED. I've been to a few of those forums and
events, and frankly, they're not even close to what I've
experienced over these last few years.

The place I am talking about is more like Plato's cave
than the red circle on the TED stage. My amazing mentors did not speak to me for 18 minutes and then disappear into the ether; they sat across from me, literally and
virtually, and brought me out from the shadows into the
light of real knowledge. How did this happen? I'm still not
entirely sure, but there is one thing I know beyond any
doubt: They fired my passion to sit across from you,
through the pages of this book, and share their teachings
with you.

I've come to call this place the School of Greatness.

It's not your stereotypical school. There are no class-rooms. No homework. No principal or dean enforcing rules or even tracking attendance. Nobody pays tuition (except maybe the price of this book). Some of the "pro-fessors" would recoil at being called that. And when we leave to try our hands at the real world once again, there will definitely be no graduation ceremony and certainly no diploma.

Now to be clear, this school is great not because it admits only great students but because the teachers are and the students want to be. Both share big dreams. And as Wilma Rudolph, the Olympic champion who was once the fastest woman in the world, said, "Never underesti-mate the power of dreams and the influence of the human spirit. We are all the same in this notion: The potential for greatness lives within each of us."

With *The School of Greatness,* you will learn how to recognize and harness this potential. You will come to understand the importance of dreams and the tools that exist within you to make those dreams reality. *The School of Greatness* is not a bag of tricks and hacks. It's not a boot camp. It's a way of life, a way of living. When you want to lose weight and keep it off, you don't go on a diet, because diets are about artificial restriction. They're miserable. Instead, you change your lifestyle to match your goals. This is the same thing. *The School of Greatness* is a life-style for a lifetime that you are going to love.

Like the professors and students in *The School of Greatness,* I've chased big dreams my whole life. Ever since I can remember, I wanted to be an All-American

athlete. Growing up in Ohio, and then growing to be
6 foot 4, obviously meant football at the Ohio State University. That was every Ohio boy's dream. Everything I
did as I grew up was aimed toward accomplishing that
goal. There wasn't a day that went by that I didn't think
about it and work on it—and I made it, sort of. I went to a
smaller Ohio college after I transferred schools a couple
of times for better (and bigger) opportunities, and I even
set a number of records along the way. But it wasn't until
my fourth year that I finally became an All-American athlete—in the decathlon, of all things: a sport I'd never even
trained for. Never in my wildest dreams could I have
imagined that happening!

As soon as being an All-American became a reality—
first as a decathlete, then the next year, finally, in football—it immediately began to lose its luster, and I had no
idea why. I'd accomplished all of my goals, and I went
further than most people would have ever expected, but
that was little consolation. At a party celebrating my
achievements, the moment that should have been my
greatest triumph, I was miserable. I couldn't enjoy it
because my focus had already shifted to bigger and better things: turning pro. Eventually, I had a tryout in front
of a dozen NFL scouts at an indoor training facility at the
Ohio State University, my former dream school, along
with a number of future NFL players, including an even-
tual Super Bowl MVP. I performed well, but coming from
a smaller school, I had little chance of being drafted.
An Arena Football League team—which is technically
professional football—did pick me up, but 1 year is all

I played as my career ended due to a series of frustrating injuries and recovery setbacks.

Suddenly, those dreams of glory and fame came crashing down to earth. It wasn't pretty. I was 24 years old, washed up, broke, and sleeping on my sister's couch with my arm in a cast and a mountain of credit card debt staring me in the face. My dreams vanished. What I was living through at that point was a nightmare—and I feared that it was something I'd never wake up from. It was the lowest low I've ever experienced.

What I realize now, only in painful hindsight, is that I wasn't chasing the specific dream of being an All-American or playing in the NFL. Those were discrete goals. I was chasing a broader dream: being great. And what was missing from my life, on that couch with a broken wrist and no money to my name, wasn't talent or ability—it was a sense of a greater purpose, a feeling that I was working and striving for something bigger than myself.

I knew I wanted to be better, and I had all this passion and energy, but I had no outlet for it. I had to do something. So I reached out to others: friends of mine, friends of my family, coaches, my siblings. A new mentor suggested I check out LinkedIn, the social media Web site, which back then in 2008 was just starting to get traction among business professionals. I saw all sorts of potential to connect with high-profile business owners and other CEOs whom I never would've encountered otherwise. I began reaching out and connecting like a madman. I reached out specifically to people who worked in the sports business because I had just come from my own athletic experiences. I had a positive message to share, and I enjoyed helping people and relished becoming what Malcolm Gladwell calls a "connector."

I eventually built this presence on LinkedIn into an incredibly lucrative speaking, advising, and teaching business. I had no background in online business, but I had good instincts and was willing to work my butt off, and as I took some advice from mentors, the money started flowing in. After an initial period of figuring it all out, my first year brought in close to $1 million in sales. By year 3, that had more than doubled. Eventually, my business partner bought me out in a deal for seven figures.

There I was, not even 30, with more money than I'd ever seen before, having turned a vision into a lucrative reality and reinvented myself as an entrepreneur in the process. With some help and some hustle, here I was again, on top of the world. It should have been another moment of triumph—I had built a business from scratch and grown it to scale—and yet the call to something larger still haunted me. I knew a piece was missing.

One of my teachers, the author and journalist Steven Kotler, would later define greatness as "waking up every day and saying 'Okay. Today I'm going to move mountains.'" That's what I wanted. That's who I wanted to be.

I started over again, this time with the notion that I would seek out something larger, since it wasn't coming to me through these stereotypical markers of success. In January 2013, I decided that I would start interviewing some of the smartest, most successful, and *greatest* men and women in the world and ask them every question I could. I wanted to be around only those people who understood what it meant to strive for true greatness, who woke up every morning to move their respective mountains, pay it forward, and help others get to a better place. Part of my motivation was selfish—my own insatiable thirst for understanding how individuals seek and achieve this higher ground—but I also wanted to give readers and listeners access to this wisdom. What good was greatness if I couldn't share it?

The response was overwhelming. My little podcast, *The School of Greatness,* amassed a large audience with more than five million downloads before the first 2 years and hundreds of thousands of unique visitors every month. In a world with a seemingly infinite supply of available podcasts, *The School of Greatness* has been featured on the main page section of iTunes more than 10 times and has ranked number one on iTunes' Business and Health list.

Not only were these lessons resonating with listeners and readers but, as I was in the process of conveying them, they were also changing my life. They were the lessons I wish I had been given and understood when I was 16 years old, struggling to make sense of athletic gifts and struggling through a tense and often terrible family life. It's what I wished I could have turned to when, immediately after leaving the All-American podium, I was engulfed by depression and pain. They could have helped me make the most of my opportunity in professional sports—and they could have saved me hundreds of thousands of dollars in costly business mistakes.

Those lessons form the core of this book. The lessons
in this book are not *my* lessons; they are my lecture notes
from a unique and wonderful school. I'm simply lucky
enough to be the messenger. As I was writing, I learned
that there is a long tradition of this kind of book. From
Aristotle's *Ethics* and Epictetus' *Discourses* more than
2,000 years ago to a more recent book like Peter Thiel's
Zero to One, the great thinkers themselves didn't write
those books: A student did. What survived was simply
the lecture notes from an epic course we were not fortunate enough to have attended in person. Classicists have
been kind enough to give author credit to the masters,
and I hope you'll see that with this book, too. Although
my name is on the cover, the names of my teachers should
be as well. I couldn't have written this without them, and
it is with the deepest gratitude that I share their wisdom.

INTRODUCTION

What Does It Take to Be Great?

Greatness is a spiritual condition worthy to excite love, interest, and admiration; and the outward proof of possessing greatness is that we excite love, interest, and admiration.

—Matthew Arnold

I'm a pretty good athlete, but there are legions who are far better than I'll ever be. Olympic gymnast Shawn Johnson accomplished more in sports as a teenager than I will in my entire life. I've done very well in business, but men like Angel Martinez, CEO of the billion-dollar shoe brand Deckers, and fellow lifestyle entrepreneur and angel investor Tim Ferriss aren't looking in their rearview mirrors for me. So I am not just talking about the kind of greatness that can be measured and assessed by a universal standard; I am talking about the greatness of exploring, reaching, and sustaining your potential—that is, the kind of individual and unique greatness that we are all capable of.

Greatness, as I've come to learn from people like Shawn, is "not just holding a gold medal at the top of a podium." It's about inspiring people, about sharing a message, about believing the truth in that cliché: It's the journey, not the destination to some perceived treasure or moment of adulation. In fact, there are a million ways to be great and a million more things to be great at. Most of them don't come with a medal or a giant check. Consider this list.

Being a parent	Being an advocate
Being an artist	Being healthy
Being generous	Being an entrepreneur
Being a leader	Being of service
Being a change maker	

All of these are amazing dreams where greatness is a worthy and attainable goal. Those who have become great at any of them—irrespective of plaques on their walls or trophies on their mantels—are the people we can all learn from. In this book, we're going to learn from people who did stand on podiums—literally and figuratively—but were great at these things as well. They embodied excellence in many facets of their lives, and we can apply their approach to our own.

As Shawn put it to me, "Greatness means having pride in yourself, being happy with yourself, knowing you've worked for something and couldn't have done anything more. That is greatness itself." It is cultivating the character and habits that not only lead to success but also help you overcome any challenge or adversity. It's about lifting yourself up from the depths of despair and using mindfulness, joy, and love to harness your dreams. It is a progression through a series of lessons—eight areas of focus and continual improvement.

1. **Create a vision.** Most great athletes describe their ability to visualize the outcome they desire in a competition. They know what they want and where they want to go. It is as much a part of their process as any aspect of training. As the famed acting coach Lee Strasberg put it, "If we cannot see the possibility of greatness, how can we dream it?" Now, what is *your* dream?

2. **Turn adversity into advantage.** It's hard to find the story of someone who has achieved greatness who did not face some sort of significant adversity. When you look more closely, you see that this adversity actually helped them—it put them on the path toward a unique and individual form of greatness. What challenges do you face and how can you use them to develop greatness?

3. **Cultivate a champion's mindset.** What does it take to become a champion, and how does a champion see the world that she is trying to conquer? Visualization, meditation, mindfulness, and emotional intelligence are tools that help you understand who you are and where you are at any given moment in your life and allow you to find joy and fulfillment in the moment. This is where greatness takes root. How can you view the world through the eyes of a champion?

4. **Develop hustle.** We all face obstacles and seem to have an impossible amount we need to get done. Many get stuck at this wall, but what separates the greats from the rest of us is that they reduce the wall to a barrier and make it into something they can climb over. It's also important to never stop

hustling—even after we've accomplished a goal. Where will your hustle and energy come from?

5. **Master your body.** No one chooses the body they're born with, but almost everyone has the ability to build and maintain their physical assets far beyond what they imagined. It's all about thinking like a champion, training like a champion, and eating like a champion. Are you taking care of yourself?

6. **Practice positive habits.** How many hours *exactly* does it take to achieve mastery and greatness? It's not about a number, but great things will happen if you practice a certain skill over and over again. Building positive habits is a necessity to achieve your desired goals. And having a deep belief in something that can support those habits, be it religion or community or family, is a key ingredient in the recipe for greatness. What positive habits can you add to your daily life?

7. **Build a winning team.** You can't achieve greatness alone, period. Success is a shared process. Finding the right mentor and making the best use of that mentor or coach is a requirement. So is building a team of partners, employees, supporters, and fans. Success is all about developing and cultivating healthy and fruitful relationships—not just with your peers on the field of endeavor but also with those who can truly challenge you—in all aspects of your life. Whom do you need to join forces with?

8. **Be of service to others.** Trophies and rings and fat bank accounts have a surprisingly short shelf life when it comes to greatness. Research has shown

that the happiest and most thriving people are those who spend their time giving back, helping others, and participating actively in their communities. In fact, the best gifts are the ones you give; they make your own achievements that much more fulfilling. How are you going to contribute and help others?

This book is the distillation of the eight master lessons on greatness that I have discovered on my journey, with help from my network of mentors and coaches, colleagues and teachers. By studying greatness this way, we will learn that it is a process of continuous education and self-realization. It's something we'll follow for the rest of our lives.

If you're like some of my podcast listeners or a lot of people who read books such as this one, you are probably saying to yourself, "This all sounds well and good, but what is this book actually going to help me do?" That's a fair question. I'm not here to waste your time or make false promises.

What *The School of Greatness* is going to teach you is, first and foremost, what is great and special about you. Most people think greatness or being great is external to themselves, that it's something you acquire or add on. That is not true. Greatness is something that is unearthed and cultivated from within. The lessons and the teachers in *The School of Greatness* will help you find the greatness in you.

This book will then inspire you to pursue it. It'll show you how to be great—whether you're an athlete, an entrepreneur, a mom, an organizer, a freelancer, or a designer—at whatever passion you harbor deep inside. They say "seeing is believing," but sometimes even that isn't enough. Sometimes people need to be convinced. They need to be inspired to have a vision, let alone pursue it with vigor in the face of countless unseen obstacles. I was fortunate enough to have truly great men and women draw out whatever potential I have inside me, and now you and I and all the other readers are going to work to become the best we can be—together.

GROUNDING

Before I do pretty much anything in life, I like to have what I call a "grounding" moment. I originally experienced this process in sports. Before every game, the coach would prepare us for the battle ahead by getting our thoughts together and putting us in the right frame of mind. I call it getting grounded. This is where I commit myself to my vision, get connected to who I am, and focus on what I'm intending to create in that moment. You may already have grounding moments in your daily life and not even realize it. Whether it's meditating in the morning to get ready for the day, taking a moment of silence or saying a prayer before meals, or psyching yourself up mentally and physically before a game or a speech or a sales pitch or any of the other "big" moments we go through in life, it's extremely important to find some head space for whatever your ritual may be.

This grounding process is critical for your success in applying the lessons in this book to your life—and critical for success, period. If you don't give yourself a moment to visualize the clear results you want to create, then you are less likely to achieve what you desire. It's all about setting your intentions for what you want. Getting grounded can be one of the most powerful things you do if you apply this process to your daily life.

Each chapter will begin with my personal grounding statements to let you know what my intention is for you to get out of that chapter and to prepare you for what's to come. When my coaches would ground us before big games, it always gave me that calm confidence I needed to take on some of my most challenging competitors. I want to pass that calm confidence on to you. You have challenges and obstacles that stand in your way on a daily basis, and grounding in the morning and before any big moment is a habit that I know will support you tremendously.

The School of Greatness, in all its parts, is a framework for achieving real, sustainable, repeatable success. This book isn't just about making you feel warm and fuzzy. It's about giving you the tools, knowledge, and actionable resources to take your vision and turn it into a reality.

Who are you?
What do you stand for?
What's your dream?
What type of legacy do you want to create?
How can we become great together?

GET GROUNDED

In this chapter on vision, I want you to dream. Allow yourself to clear your mind and look at everything as a possibility—no dream is too big or too crazy. Imagine what you'd want your life to look like if you knew you could never fail. Let go of what someone else wants for you, what you think society wants for you, and what you think you are supposed to do because it's reasonable and "makes sense." You are here to live an extraordinary life. Think about what *you* want to do in your life and how *you* want to live.

The lessons in this chapter give you permission to design the life you've always dreamed of while living unapologetically. The exercises at the end will help you practice the lessons and exercises in the seven chapters that follow this one. If you're like I used to be, you might be tempted to skip these exercises because they seem like "work"—but that's the whole point. This can be an uncomfortable process, but it's one that finally shows you what life could be like if you choose to live in a world where "anything is possible."

Get ready, my friend. This is the beginning of a beautiful journey, and I'll be with you every step of the way.

CHAPTER 1

CREATE A VISION

The only thing worse than being blind
is having sight but no vision.
—**Helen Keller**

Greatness is my passion, but vision is my obsession. Let me explain. A clear vision can unleash extraordinary, mind-boggling power. I've been known to get more than a little intense on this topic. Let me tell you a story about a guy I met named Steve who reminded me of my younger self and was probably like a lot of you out there. He had been friends with my girlfriend at the time for a number of years, and she wanted us to meet up over dinner. I went through the whole "where are you from, what do you do" small-talk racket that you do when you meet new people, and Steve told me he was in graduate school to be a doctor of physical therapy and was finishing up in the next 6 months. As an athlete who has been through his fair share of injuries, I am familiar with physical therapy, so I found this pretty interesting.

I asked him, "So Steve, what do you want to do after you graduate? What's the dream?"

Like most people who just got blindsided on a first friend date, he said, "I'm not really sure."

"Well, if you could have anything, what would you want? If you could have it all, what would it be?"

Steve started talking about working with the military and doing physical therapy on wounded veterans and enlisted soldiers. The benefits would be good, and he could support his family. There's a big military hospital in Germany, so maybe they could see some of the world that way, too.

"That's really cool," I said. "Has that been what you've always wanted, or is there something else?"

Very quickly, Steve said, "I used to be a football coach. So I'd love to be a physical therapist on a pro sports team and work on these great athletes."

Now he was speaking about something I knew well, and I could tell he meant it. "That's awesome, Steve. So is that what you really want?"

He thought about it and said, "You know, actually, it'll probably be a lot of hours, like 80 hours a week. And I'd have to work my way up. And it'd be a lot of time and energy. So maybe working for a pro team is just one of my options, like plan B or C."

"Okay, so you don't want to work for a pro team?" Now I was confused. "Then what is it you really, really *want*? What's your vision?"

I laugh every time I think back to this dinner conversation, because I feel so bad for Steve. When he ordered his meal, he had no idea it came with a side of interrogation, especially from someone who seemed to be getting frustrated with him. And believe me, I was getting frustrated, because I was asking him to focus in on what he really wanted to do with his life—what he desired—and instead, like so many of us who have not yet recognized the inherent potential for greatness within ourselves, he was listing all the things he could do but probably wouldn't.

I learned about desire—the distinction between what we *can* do and what we *want* to do—and how to uncover it from the unstoppable Danielle LaPorte. She's a phenomenal motivational speaker and author who has graced us with her presence on *The School of Greatness* podcast a couple of times. The first time she came on, she said something that still spins around in my head to this day. She stated, "You need desire to be fully alive and you need vision to fulfill your desires." How amazing is that?!

Together with *The Desire Map: A Guide to Creating Goals with Soul,* which she published in 2014, Danielle changed my perspective on vision and is mostly responsible for turning it from an interest to an obsession. And now, every time we speak, she hones and clarifies my understanding of vision and desire a little more. The last time, she described her book this way: "*The Desire Map* is about helping as many people as possible get clear on their core desired feelings."

That was exactly what I was trying to do with Steve: pushing him to get clear on how he felt about life so he could figure out what he truly wanted to do. Finally, he got real: "To have my own practice by the beach. And work like 5 hours a day. And then be able to be there to support my family."

That is a vision—it was practical, it was real, and though he'd been afraid to be direct about it earlier, now you could hear the sincerity in his voice. I was eager to ask him how he felt after saying that out loud, but I didn't want his dinner to get cold, so I let it go until dessert. We all dug into our entrées, and, between bites, Steve added one final thought that sums up the entire reason that holds people back from excelling in the School of Greatness:

"I just don't know if that's possible."

Yes, it is absolutely possible, and it has nothing to do with ability. As the renowned leadership expert John Maxwell says, "Successful and unsuccessful people do not vary greatly in their abilities. They vary in their *desires* to reach their potential." (emphasis mine) The reason I know this is true and that Steve's dream is possible is because of my time with one of the School of Greatness's greatest teachers: Angel Martinez.

I met Angel Martinez in Goleta, California, at the new headquarters of his company, Deckers Brands, a fast-growing, billion-dollar global footwear company. I'd heard of Deckers from the same mentor who introduced me to the power of LinkedIn, but I had little understanding of the company's size or track record before connecting with Angel, Deckers' CEO. From the looks of the company's beautiful new campus, with its glass walls, intricate woodwork, and gleaming granite floors, it was doing pretty well. It turns out, like millions of other people, I was more familiar with two of their best-selling brands: UGG and Teva. When you think about the uniqueness of those two shoes and then you meet Angel, a guy who looks more like a jazz musician than a CEO, you understand why his motto for Deckers is "We want to inspire the unconventional."

Angel took an unconventional route to greatness. It would be difficult to find another CEO with a similar résumé and worldview. An iconoclast and footwear industry legend, Angel was a founding member of Reebok—its third employee—and the catalyst for the company's explosive growth back in the 1980s. He single-handedly pushed Reebok into the budding aerobics marketplace by combining style with function and designing the world's first aerobic shoe for women. Driven by sales of that shoe (called the Freestyle) and lines of improved tennis, running, and basketball shoes, Reebok became the fastest-growing company in history up to that time and blew past Nike for the dominant position in the US athletic shoe market.

Angel went on to serve as CEO of the Rockport Company, a Reebok subsidiary, before eventually leaving the footwear giant to pursue his own ideas and passions. He later helped found Keen, the popular outdoor footwear brand, and joined Deckers as CEO in 2005, when the company had $200 million in sales. Under Angel's watch, in less than a decade Deckers' revenues have soared to nearly $1.5 billion. Fueled by his entrepreneurial vision,

the company has expanded around the world with popular retail outlets, new brands, and record growth. If
greatness is built upon insight, acquired wisdom, and a
unique vision, Angel is the embodiment of that path to
success—a path that begins in prerevolutionary Cuba.

Born in Cuba in 1955, Angel was sent off to live with
guardians in New York when he was a toddler, never to
return to his native country and never to live with his
father or mother again. His mother had left her young
family when Angel was born, and because of the revolu-
tion in 1959, Angel would not see his father again for 34
years. Raised in a tenement in the South Bronx by his
elderly aunt and her disabled husband, Angel always felt
like an outsider who never quite fit in.

His first brush with footwear envy came when he
was in grade school and yearned for a pair of Converse
Chuck Taylor All Star high-top sneakers, the Air Jordans
of the day. To be cool, you had to have Cons. At $6.99 a
pair, they may as well have cost a million dollars. His aunt
offered to pay $1.99 for sneakers—the price of cheap
sneakers at Woolworth's—but Angel was determined to
get his Cons. He collected bottles that he redeemed at
two cents apiece until he earned enough for them. So precious were those shoes to him that he walked the four
blocks home from the shoe store on the sides of his feet
so as not to get the bottoms of the Cons dirty.

"It was a moment of epiphany, the perfect confluence
of attaining something I'd dreamed about for a long time
and having it turn out to be just as good if not better than
I had hoped for," Angel recalled. "It was my first taste of

the power of a product to provide emotional and psychological comfort."

LESSON #1:
BE SPECIFIC

This was also Angel's first positive lesson in the power of vision. More important, it was a lesson in the power of a clear, specific vision. He didn't want just any shoes. He didn't ask his aunt for "a cool pair of shoes." He knew exactly what he wanted: the $6.99 top-of-the-line Converse Chuck Taylor All Star sneakers in the iconic black canvas with white laces and toe guard. He dreamed about these shoes so vividly that he could feel them on his feet and would do nearly anything to have them.

As the award-winning Brazilian novelist Paulo Coelho wrote in his bestseller *The Alchemist*, "People are capable, at any time in their lives, of doing what they dream of." And it's that much easier to accomplish when you know exactly what your dream is. It might seem odd to you that a goal as small as having a pair of nice sneakers of his own would be considered a dream—most of us have never had to struggle so hard for such a small material possession—but for Angel, growing up poor in the Bronx, it put him on the path he followed the rest of his life.

Angel's story blew me away. From my time in the business world after college, I always knew vision was important, but to see the power of a clear vision on one person's life like that was a transformative moment for me. Not only did it guide him toward achieving that first small dream—as a kid, no less—it shaped his entire life. If Angel hadn't obsessed over his Cons to the point that he collected two-cent bottles for months in order to buy his first pair for himself, would he have ended up in the shoe business? Would he have become a founding employee of Reebok or the CEO of Deckers? Probably not. Such is the power of a clear, early vision.

After talking with Angel, I started thinking about my own past. Did I have a big, outsize dream that I was obsessed with while growing up in suburban Ohio? What were my $6.99 Cons? Then it hit me. As I talked with Angel, the entire memory came back to me in a giant flash. I was 6 or 7 years old, sitting on the living room sofa with my dad watching an Ohio State football game. I don't remember who they were playing or who won, but I remember the announcers talking about an Ohio State linebacker named Chris Spielman who'd graduated the year before and been chosen by the Detroit Lions in the second round of the NFL Draft. They said he was a two-time All-American. I had never heard that phrase before.

"Dad, what's an All-American?" I asked.

"They're the best players in all of college," he answered nonchalantly, unaware of the future impact of what he was about to say. "There are only a few of them. They make all the big plays."

Wow, I thought, *one of the guys from my favorite team is one of the best in the entire country?!*

I remember sitting there staring into the television, listening to these announcers talk with energy and passion about Spielman and the other All-Americans on the field that day. *Who are these guys? What makes them so special?*

For those unschooled in the splendor and glory that is Ohio State football, here's a quick lesson. Practically the entire state shuts down on Saturdays in the fall when the Buckeyes play. Their stadium, called the Horseshoe, holds more than 100,000 people, and it's always filled to capacity with screaming fans dressed in scarlet and gray. Many of them are wearing the jerseys of All-American Buckeyes past and present. They're all there, I realized, to see these All-Americans—guys like Chris Spielman—do amazing things and lead their team to victory.

At such a young age, I didn't have the words to describe that feeling, but in that moment, I became obsessed with greatness in sports. I wanted to be like all those All-Americans. I wanted to be *one of the best.* I wanted to be great. Thinking back to that day and then to all the years of practices, workouts, eating regimens, supplement experimentation, games, injuries, and physical therapy sessions, I realized becoming an All-American wasn't just an idea that popped into my head one day. It was the name for the dream I'd had since I was a little kid.

Like Angel's dream for his first pair of shoes, being an All-American can sound a little silly or even a little cute if you don't have the context and you don't know how that singular vision guided decades of our lives. Having a goal that feels attainable but slightly out of reach provides focus and direction. It prevents you from getting distracted or discouraged when things don't go your way. Angel wanted those Cons as soon as humanly possible, but seven dollars' worth of bottles at two cents a pop is a lot of bottles for a little kid. I wanted to be an All-American, but I had no idea how to go about doing it, and neither did anyone I knew. It wasn't as if that kind of greatness was living next door, the way that Steve Jobs lived near the famous Packard's garage or the way it might be for a kid who hopes to succeed his father as CEO of a family business or graduate from the college his parents went to. Our goals felt outsize to those around us, and our timelines were different, but they both were well defined with a clear end point. If you want to be great at anything, you've got to have a clear vision of exactly what you want, why you want it, and when you want it to happen.

All greats do this, including the greats you will hear much more from over the course of the rest of this book. It was an essential component to Shawn Johnson climbing the medal stand in Beijing, Kyle Maynard climbing Mount Kilimanjaro, Rich Roll going from overweight lawyer to world-class ultramarathoner, Scooter Braun building one of the most successful music management firms in the industry, and my brother climbing the ranks of the world's great jazz musicians, to name a few. Now, having a vision isn't all you need to be great, happy, or successful, but it's absolutely true that you can't be those things without one.

LESSON #2:
LET YOUR VISION BE YOUR IDENTITY

We focused first on creating a vision because it's the most important step to getting anywhere and achieving anything you want in any area of life. But we also have to be clear about what a vision is. A vision is not just a dream. A powerful vision emerges when we couple our dreams with a set of clear goals. Without both, we are apt to wander in a clueless and purposeless fog, because a dream without goals is just a fantasy. And fantasies are the bad kind of visions—the hallucinogenic kind, not the real kind.

A powerful vision emerges when we couple our dreams with a set of clear goals.

Without a real vision, we lack identity. Having a real vision isn't just about clarifying what you want; it's about defining what and who you want to be. My vision was to achieve All-American status when I was younger, but what I really wanted to *be* was great.

For Angel, the Cons were about being like all the other kids—being equal—at a point in his life when he felt unlike any of them. Most of us can relate to wanting something stylish that our friends have, but few of us can probably understand what it's like to literally and figuratively struggle with identity from such an early age. On Angel's first day of school, his guardian introduced him to the principal as Angelo, even though that wasn't his name. In the 1950s in New York City, it was easier to get by if people thought you were Italian rather than Cuban. It wasn't until he was on his own in college that he could finally convince people to call him what he wanted to be called.

"I just made up my mind," he told me. "'No, that's not my name. Angel is my name. You can call me 'angel' until you figure out how to pronounce my name, but I'll make it easy for you and just give it to you. It's Angel [An-hel]. I'm not even asking you to do it with an accent or anything.'"

But it was about more than people pronouncing his name correctly; it was about making a life. Having his own name was something he needed. He craved becoming someone on his own terms, in line with his vision for who he was (and is to this day), not what some public school administrator said he was on a piece of paper, even if his guardian had the best of intentions. See, what might seem conventional to some of us today—the idea of going to college, getting a good job, having a nice house—was, for someone with Angel's background, not just unconventional but downright crazy when he was growing up. Especially if he insisted on embracing his Cuban immigrant heritage just as the Cold War really started getting chilly.

Listening to Angel talk about his childhood made this distinction clear to me. It revealed a relentless ambition, a life of striving for true accomplishment. To be equal, to be somebody, to be great. But not great in the more traditional, achievement-based way that I was trying to be great. His was greatness in life, in living.

It might seem like Angel had two completely different visions—one to be just like everybody else, the other to be his own man—but actually they are two sides of the same coin. They unify what he wants with who he wants to be. That is the essence of identity. Just as pairing your dreams with your goals is the essence of a real vision, unifying your vision lets you blow past what other people think your limitations are. Beyond those limitations is where greatness lives. If you don't figure out what you want in life and who you want to be, you will most likely feel trapped within those limitations. No path to greatness has ever involved settling for less than what you really want.

Let's go back to the dinner where I met Steve. Steve thought his dream was to be a physical therapist, maybe with the military or a pro sports team. In fact, his dream was to live near the beach and work from home a few hours each day so he could always be there for his family. No wonder he was confused. He wasn't sure it was possible because he didn't realize that being a physical therapist wasn't his dream; it was just a goal on the path and a means to achieving his actual dream. What he was after was control over his life and the luxury of seeing his kids grow up. Once you clarify this, then it becomes possible to develop a real plan for getting there.

"The challenge," Angel told me as we discussed his childhood, "is to be able to project yourself into a future that you have no reference point for. If you grew up in a

well-to-do, solidly middle-class family where you got a
new car, you lived in a nice house, you took a nice vacation once in a while—I'm not talking about anything
exotic, I'm talking about the middle-class American
dream—well, for me growing up, that was absolute fanta-
syland. That was something I saw on TV, on *Leave It to
Beaver.* That house on TV was a palace to me, and it was a
challenge to convince myself that I belonged there, too."

The famed World War II general and French president
Charles de Gaulle is reported to have said, "Greatness is a
road leading towards the unknown." And he was right, but
only in a particular sense, I think. It's not that you don't
know what it looks like; the unknown part is what it's
like to *be there.* This is something so many of the students
in the School of Greatness—myself included—struggle
with when we first get started. Greatness is for those
people over there—they've been there and done that.
They deserve it for whatever reason. Who am I? What
have I done to think I can achieve these great things?
I'm just Lewis from Ohio or Steve from LA or Angel from
the Bronx.

LESSON #3:
TURN THE TELESCOPE AROUND

The key is to understand that the vision creation process
doesn't end when you've clearly articulated what your
dreams and goals are. There is another part to it—the
part where you envision what it's like to have achieved
those goals and live that dream. I learned this, too, from
Angel Martinez.

"When I was a kid, I came up with this idea while playing with a telescope," he told me. "I realized that you could look through both ends. When you look through the small end, everything is far away. But when you look through the big end, you say, 'Wow, that looks totally different when I turn the telescope around.' I would tell people who doubted themselves, 'You might just be looking at your life through the wrong end of the telescope.'"

Could you have the same problem? That outsize dream that seems so far away is often a lot closer than you think. It just seems distant because we look through the wrong end. Angel's point of view was so absolute and so unusual that it made me reconsider my own story. Then he said something that struck a chord:

"I came to the conclusion that it's easier to come from a place than to go to a place. At Reebok, I thought we were better than Nike," he recalled. "We just hadn't done it yet. I didn't come to Deckers because I wanted to stay in the funky old building we were in before this new one was built. I was already at the other end of the telescope for this company. I saw this as a multibillion-dollar company because of the quality of the people and the products and the brands. I realized, you become what you envision yourself being."

You become what you envision yourself being. If Mike Tyson hadn't ruined face tattoos for everyone, I would tattoo that phrase backward on my forehead so I could read it every morning when I got up and I looked in the mirror. Because that is the true power of a vision on the path to greatness. It's not a destination or a specific achievement or an amount of something—it's a state of being that encompasses all of the goals you've set for yourself along the way.

You become what you envision yourself being.

One of the amazing things about doing what I do and getting to spend time with these teachers in the School of Greatness is leaving every encounter with far more wisdom than I arrived with. It's a great gift, and sharing it with the world is at the heart of my mission. It's why I've carefully chosen the stories I share with you. For instance, Angel Martinez is one of those rare individuals who could fit into pretty much every category on my list of traits that form the foundation of greatness. But I started the book with his story—a story of true vision in every sense of the word—because he is the kind of inspiring person we can all use as a reference point when we doubt our dreams or ourselves.

Angel has been driven by a vision that has propelled him out of bed every day for more than 50 years, long past the time he's earned enough money to stay in bed as late as he wants. Your job is to create a vision that makes you want to jump out of bed in the morning. If it doesn't, go back to bed until you have a bigger dream.

I have discovered and developed these powerful exercises to help you get crystal clear on what you want, why you want it, and when you want it to happen. To pursue and achieve greatness, you must truly become the author of your own destiny, and the writing starts with these four exercises.

EXERCISE #1:
Your Certificate of Achievement (COA)

Write down your goal. Print it. Frame it. Hang it somewhere you will see it. Every day.

Writing down your goal is a powerful thing. Declaring your vision and putting a date on it, as though it *will* happen (or, as Angel would say, like it already did), is even more powerful.

This exercise is about getting total clarity on what you want (like I did with Steve) and why you want it, and then declaring that vision for yourself in the next 6 months or whatever date you have in your head, as long as it's specific. Your goal can be financial, personal, or health or career related. It almost doesn't matter what the vision is. There's only one rule: It should be something hard to achieve. It must be something that terrifies you when you say it out loud to someone you respect. At the same time, it should be something that is possible to achieve in the allotted time frame—provided you put in the work. And then you write yourself a new goal once it is completed.

I am not the first person to come up with the idea to write down goals. Many who have come before me have recommended something similar. But I didn't learn this from them. I came by it honestly, at a fairly early age, watching my coaches. As an athlete, I have played on more teams with more coaches than I can count. We've been good; we've been great; we've been bad; we've been horrible. On most of those teams, the difference between success and failure was razor thin. Rarely could you put your finger on why, and God knows our coaches tried. Over time, though, I noticed one thing that distinguished the good teams from the bad ones or the successful coaches from the unsuccessful. The seasons where coaches had us write out our team vision and our personal goals were the most successful seasons I ever had. That shared vision provided a foundation for the team. Without it, we were athletes playing without greater purpose. Having that purpose and knowing why we were playing enabled the members of those teams to sacrifice for each other in ways the visionless teams never could.

The power of a clear, stated vision struck me so deeply that after my sports career was over, I wanted to see if I could apply this exercise to business and to life. I started with something that had dogged me my whole life: public speaking. I was terrified of speaking in public. I could not get up to talk in front of people to save my life. Whenever I gave speeches in school, I was a sweating, shaking, nervous wreck. I decided I never wanted to feel that way ever again.

A year removed from my professional football career after a number of injury setbacks, I joined Toastmasters International, an educational organization that helps members with their communication and public-speaking skills. I went every week for a year, with the goal of getting over my fear of speaking in public. But that goal wasn't specific enough; the vision wasn't clear enough. "Getting better" was too vague. Toward the middle of the program, excited by my progress but not satisfied with my direction, I wrote down a scary goal: Make $5,000 for a speech. What made it so frightening was the fact that I wasn't able to achieve it in that moment. There was no way anyone was going to pay me to speak at an event, not that version of me. But I knew that stepping toward my fear, that's where the magic is created. I had doubts—*Who is going to listen to a young kid like me? What do I have to offer?*—but I gave myself a deadline to do it: 9 months.

I wrote it down on a piece of paper. I framed it and hung it on my mirror where I would see it every morning when I woke up. Just like writing down our shared team vision back in my football days, framing and posting my speaking goal (with the date!) gave me a purpose and a destination. It turned my telescope around. Not only did I achieve that goal in the time allotted, but today I am much more comfortable onstage and regularly get offered upwards of $25,000 for speaking opportunities around the world. And it all started with establishing a clear vision and writing down my goals. I've been doing this exercise for more than 15 years now. I started calling it my Certificate of Achievement to make it an official part of the quest for greatness, and it continues to serve me well as both an athlete and an entrepreneur.

Download your Certificate of Achievement at schoolofgreatness.com/resources and you will receive an easy template for completing this exercise in excellence. Once complete, print out your COA, frame it, and place it where you're going to look at it every day. Make it the focal point of your daily routine, always at the top of your mind and on the tip of your tongue as that singular thing you must achieve.

EXERCISE #2:
Perfect Day Itinerary (PDI)

This may be one of the most powerful exercises you ever do for yourself, so make it count. I've coached many wandering entrepreneurs through this exercise, and most of them have told me it changed their lives. I wasn't surprised—when I did it for the first time years ago, it literally set me up for creating the life I always envisioned and living it every day.

In this exercise, your job is to map out what your perfect day looks like along the path to achieving your vision. There are two parts to this exercise: the macro and the micro. First up is the macro part, where you figure out what your perfect day would look like at a general level. Not every day is going to be exactly the same. Each day will look a little different depending on what happened the day before. It should look a little different; otherwise life would get boring and monotonous. Still, you want to have a broad sense of what each perfect day feels like. This starts with a series of questions.

How do I want every day to look?

How do I want to feel every single day?

What am I creating daily?

Whom am I spending my time with?

What places am I exposing myself to?

What passions am I fulfilling?

Take out a blank piece of paper or open a new document on your computer and fill the first half of the page with the answers, in broad terms, to these questions.

Here was mine from my first time completing the exercise.

PART 1: MY PERFECT DAY

In my perfect day, I wake up next to the woman of my dreams and she's crying tears of joy because she's so excited about the life we have together. I'm preparing to compete in the 2016 Olympics with USA Team Handball, so I head to an intense training session with my coach to increase my physical strength and athleticism. Then I'm working on my TV show that's on a major network and supporting my company team with all of my projects that inspire entrepreneurs to follow their own passions and make a living around what they love.

Now, in part 2 (the micro part), write out a detailed itinerary for the next perfect day on the bottom half of the page. This should include everything you want to do and have to do and exactly how and when you want to do it.

Every successful sports season I had included detailed daily itineraries. We received one in the morning and one before practice, and they set us up to win. There was no more wondering what to do, when to do it, or how much time to spend on it. It was all right there, plain as day, laid out in the steps necessary to reach our end goal. This is true for every professional sports team as well. The successful ones have a daily plan designed to lead them to achieve their vision. Theirs are similar, if not in many ways identical, to what I'm asking you to create.

Here is a version of my daily itinerary while I was writing this book.

PART 2: TOMORROW'S PERFECT DAY

7:30 a.m. Wake up, meditate, and enjoy the views from my balcony.

8:00 a.m. Healthy breakfast with green juice or a smoothie.

9:00 a.m. CrossFit/kickboxing or private skills training session.

10:45 a.m. Check in with my team about projects of the day.

11:00 a.m. Complete the top three tasks that were on my list before bed.

12:00 p.m. Healthy lunch at home or lunch meeting with someone who inspires me.

1:30 p.m. Back to the top three on my to-do list, recording interviews, doing videos, or working with the team.

3:00 p.m. Physical therapy to increase flexibility (2 days a week).

5:00 p.m. Pickup basketball, hiking with friends, swim in ocean.

7:30 p.m. Healthy dinner at home or out with friends.

9:00 p.m. Read, movie, events with influencers on the town.

11:00 p.m. Make a list of what I'm most grateful for today, create a "completed list" of what I did today. Write the top three list of what I want to create tomorrow.

11:30 p.m. Meditate, sleep, dream, recover body.

If you let it, the PDI can be a powerful exercise that will set your year (and many years to come) to contain the best days of your business and life.

It also helps validate your vision and vice versa. If your vision doesn't fit in with your perfect day at either the macro or micro level, you need to either change your vision or be more open, honest, and creative about what it will take at a daily level to reach your vision.

EXERCISE #3:
Personal Principles Declaration (PPD)

The third vision exercise is the statement of who you will be and what you will stand for in your life, even in the toughest moments. I call it the Personal Principles Declaration (PPD) because that's what it is—a declaration. You're not making a wish list or scribbling down some nice thoughts. You are declaring to yourself and to your world that this list of five principles is what you stand for and live by, no matter what comes your way. When something goes wrong or doesn't happen the way you envisioned, you fall back on these principles instead of falling into a negative spiral or becoming a victim of circumstances. You don't let your bruised ego get the best of you, because your vision is bigger than your ego. You will never achieve what you really want if you let your ego stand in the way of your principles.

Here is my PPD.

1. Love myself, everyone, and everything.
2. Be in service to support others and the world.
3. Always give my best and strive for greatness in everything I do.

4. Live in abundance.

5. Create a win/win with everything.

Here is Angel Martinez's PPD.

1. Tell the truth.

2. Be there for your family and friends.

3. Respect the opinions of others.

4. Know that you don't have all the answers. Ask questions.

5. Have humility.

6. Persevere.*

Print out your PPD or write it on a card and keep it in your wallet. Read over your principles often. Your ego is strong and very convincing (at least I know mine is), especially when the chips are down, but when you hold fast to your principles, you cannot be deterred on your path to achieving your vision. It doesn't matter what kind of adversity comes your way—and it will come, especially the bigger the vision—your principles are a set of powerful tools that will serve you along the journey.

*Of course, Angel added one more principle for good measure. You don't get from where he was to where he is now by doing just enough!

EXERCISE #4:
Your Personal Statement Plan (PSP)

This exercise is designed to bring everything about your vision together into a plan of action. We can think and plan and hope and wish, but until we do something about our vision (as you will see in the following chapters), it will only ever be just a dream.

On a blank piece of paper, fill out the following worksheet (to download this document, go to schoolofgreatness.com/resources).

Your name _____

Today's date _____ 6 or 12 months from today _____

Answer these questions.

Who am I? _____

_____

_____

_____

_____

What do I stand for? _____

_____

_____

_____

_____

What is my vision for myself, my family, and the world?_____

_____

_____

_____

_____

_____

List your five principles (Personal Principles Declaration)

1. _____

2. _____

3. _____

4. _____

5. _____

This is an opportunity to get clear on what you want, but make no mistake—living your vision is a commitment. It demands time and dedication, so don't take it lightly. Pause for a moment, if needed, before you put the vision of your life to paper. But make sure to complete these exercises in the next 24 hours while they're fresh in your mind.

Write out the top three goals you want to either achieve or maintain for the next 6 or 12 months under each of the following categories: family, relationships, business, money, health, recreation, spirituality/inner growth.

Below each goal, write a detailed action plan for how you will achieve that specific goal: Make it so annoyingly step-by-step and spelled out that anyone could read your plan, follow it exactly, and achieve it themselves. Here is a sample of how three categories might look.

FAMILY

GOAL #1:   VISIT PARENTS AND SIBLINGS TWICE A YEAR.

Step 1: Find time in my schedule every 6 months where I could fly home (in next 3 days).

Step 2: Call Mom, Dad, and siblings to see when they are free (in next 7 days).

Step 3: Save to my calendar the set dates we agree on and book flights (within 2 weeks).

BUSINESS

GOAL #1: **MAKE $10,000 A MONTH IN THE NEXT 6 MONTHS.**

> **Step 1:** Calculate how many customers it will take to reach this (1 day).

> **Step 2:** Break this down into how many sales this will take weekly and daily (1 day).

> **Step 3:** Set up and host one webinar per week to current prospects to generate these sales.

HEALTH

GOAL #1: **LOSE 15 POUNDS IN 60 DAYS.**

> **Step 1:** Find a workout plan I'll be excited about (within 24 hours).

> **Step 2:** Find coach or accountability partner (3 days).

> **Step 3:** Schedule workout days and times of workouts for the next 60 days (3 days).

> **Step 4:** Begin training on this plan in 4 days!

Write down the type of person you will need to be in order to accomplish this in 6 or 12 months.

Example: "I will need to be committed. Most important, I'll need to let go of the pressure or stress and empower others around me to support me instead of doing it all on my own. I'll need to deepen my understanding about business and how the world works for me to be able to flow in it effortlessly."

I will _____

_____

_____

_____

_____

Now write down the breakthroughs you will create as a result of understanding who you need to be to accomplish your goals.

Example: "Letting go of reaction or defensiveness. Peace with myself, and understanding that everything at the end of the day is 'small stuff' and doesn't require me to react in a way that doesn't serve me if things don't go well."

_____

_____

_____

_____

This is your living document that you will adjust over time. Every 6 to 12 months, you should revisit it and make sure you are on track to live your vision.

COACHING TIP

Your life matters, and so do your dreams. It's time you act like they matter. The best way to start doing that is to visualize and map out how you want your dreams to look on a day-to-day basis. The key to greatness is fulfilling what you want in your life first and being an inspiration to yourself. By creating an inspiring life that works, you inspire others around you to do the same. This ripple effect is powerful. Just imagine if everyone focused on making sure their lives were fulfilling and inspiring. What would the world look like then?! When you complete this homework, show it to a friend or someone you care about and tell them your dreams and what you stand for. Ask them to join you in completing these vision exercises as well, so you have an accountability buddy. Then post it on social media and use #SchoolOfGreatness so others in the community can support you along your journey. You've got this, and I've got your back. It's time to make magic happen, and it starts with you getting clear on exactly what you want in your life and why you want it. Let's go!

GET GROUNDED

With everything I've ever wanted in life—from wanting to be a great athlete when I was young yet getting picked last for teams to learning to start my own business from my sister's couch after a career-ending injury with no hope in sight to finding a loving relationship with my ego and insecurities getting in the way—it has always and will continue to come with an equally difficult challenge.

When adversity arises, you have two choices: (1) Do nothing, let it overwhelm you, and fall victim to your circumstances, or (2) embrace the challenge and move toward the adversity, making it part of your success story. Prepare yourself for these moments, because they are going to happen in all areas of your life whether you like it or not. When you understand this and learn to embrace adversity, then you can learn to overcome it and use it to your advantage.

When I face challenges in my life, I think about my friend Kyle Maynard, whom I write about in this chapter, and how he, along with others, shows me how much I have to be grateful for.

CHAPTER 2

TURN ADVERSITY INTO ADVANTAGE

Storms make trees take deeper roots.

—Dolly Parton

For most of us, it's difficult to imagine becoming a championship wrestler, a football player, a weight lifter, a mixed martial arts fighter, or a mountain climber. There are so many obstacles that stand in the way of each of those goals: money, opportunity, coaching, talent and ability, confidence. Any one of them could derail these impressive dreams at any time.

Now imagine becoming *all* those things before you cut the cake on your 30th birthday. A friend of mine did. His name is Kyle Maynard, and he is one of the most inspiring teachers I've ever met. When he was a young man, those physical feats I just listed were only a few of the goals on his bucket list—a bucket that would never go empty and would one day include inspiring others to do great things. Kyle wanted to achieve his goals as badly as any person who aspired to greatness has wanted something. And by the middle of 2012, at the age of 26, he'd accomplished all of them. He played football in middle school. He was a champion wrestler in high school and won 36 varsity wrestling matches during his senior year. He fought a full three-round mixed martial arts (MMA) fight. He climbed the nearly 20,000-foot Mount Kilimanjaro.

On their own, these might not sound like particularly lofty goals. I've met many other people who achieved these same dreams at a much higher level, yet none of them did it the way Kyle did. When they did it, ESPN didn't award them with two ESPYs for their accomplishments, the way the network did in Kyle's case. Why? Kyle's accomplishments stand head and shoulders above those of most other men his age—most other men, period— because Kyle himself stands only 3 feet 8 inches tall. He is a congenital amputee. A birth defect related to something called amniotic band syndrome deprived him of the fully formed arms and legs that most of us take for granted. As he describes it: "Basically, my arms end right where your elbows would be. For each arm, they're both about the same length, and my legs end slightly above where the knee is, and I have two feet. They're just a little bit different."

Amniotic band syndrome occurs when the blood clots in utero and fibrous bands constrict the growth of fetal limbs. Doctors have no idea why it happens or what causes it, but they peg the statistical chances of it happening in an otherwise normal pregnancy at 1 in 10 million. Growing up, Kyle did not just face the typical external obstacles all of us face at one time or another; he dealt with a whole unique set of struggles that were a part of his life from the day he was born. And yet he accomplished each of the things he had envisioned for himself.

IT'S ALL IN THE DOING

You should not feel bad for Kyle Maynard. Pity isn't a feeling he's searching for. What I learned from Kyle over the course of our talks brought my understanding of goals and greatness into a kind of focus I'd never had before. Creating a vision is about clearly defining what you want (your goals) and who you want to be (your dreams). But goals and vision are one thing—they are made in our minds. They are only hypotheticals. Anyone can tell themselves they have a vision for what they want to create in the world, but it is our actions that dictate what we create in reality, where anything can (and does) happen. It is in the doing that the goals become real.

To be good at something requires talent, vision, and action. Greatness is what remains when that talent and vision meet adversity—and persist in the face of it. This is what makes Kyle a great teacher, and it's why he can teach us more than just about anyone about overcoming adversity on the path to greatness. When it comes to greatness, he teaches us that there is no room in life for excuses:

"When I was younger, when I was 10 years old, I used to cry myself to sleep some nights because I would just wish that I would wake up and have arms and legs. And no matter how hard I would have focused on that forever, it never would have happened. So when we go and focus on those things that we have no control over, it brings us nothing but unhappiness."

This mindset is unsustainable and unproductive in the face of adversity. It gets us nowhere. How does that old saying go: "Wish in one hand, crap in the other, and see which one fills up first"? That was a reality Kyle was forced to reckon with at an early age. As he said, no amount of focus or wishing was going to change anything. Like many of the breakthrough moments I've had in my life around the issue of adversity, Kyle's aha moment came on the football field. He was 11 years old.

"I made my first tackle in a football game when I was 11," Kyle recalled. "It seems like a relatively simple thing, but my life changed forever in that moment. I stopped having so many concerns over what might happen in the distant future. I stopped being consumed with wondering what I would do with my life. I used to ask questions like 'Would I have to live at home with Mom and Dad forever?' 'Would I ever have a girlfriend or a job someday?' And the interesting part: It wasn't like I was given any answers to any of those questions. I was just playing football."

Kyle wasn't thinking or worrying or wishing, he was *doing.* At 11 years old, no less! It was in the action and the perseverance in the face of tall odds that obstacles started to dissolve and he took his first concrete steps toward greatness. It became almost a philosophy of adversity, one that he lived by from that day forward.

"My life has had its challenges since that tackle," he told me. "But the concerns and fears I had over the future continued to subside until they became relatively nonexistent. I mostly attribute that to putting myself in situations where I'm uncomfortable and staying with it until I become comfortable.

"When I was 19, I gave a speech to several thousand of the world's most successful business owners, sandwiched between then senator Obama and Dr. Steven Covey, best-selling author of *The Seven Habits of Highly Effective People*. Once I gave that talk, it's no wonder every speech since then has been a whole lot easier!"

Amazing! Think about that for a second: In 8 years, Kyle went from crying himself to sleep every night, wondering if he'd ever have a girlfriend or a job or a place of his own, to speaking to a room full of business luminaries between the future president of the United States and the author of one of the most successful self-help business books of all time. And it all started with a tackle on the football field—with one little action.

"We are our greatest ally in terms of our capability to get past adversity. We can be incredibly motivated," Kyle often says. It all lies in how we perceive and engage the adversity we face.

THE LANGUAGE OF INTERNAL ADVERSITY

One of the things it took me a long time to learn about adversity, especially in my own life, is that adversity isn't always external or physical. In fact, it usually isn't. I first started to understand this through my work on emotional intelligence with Chris Lee (whom we'll meet next chapter), but it wasn't until I sat down to talk with Nicole Lapin about money that my eyes opened to how broadly adversity can manifest itself in our lives.

Nicole is a finance expert who spent years as a reporter and anchor for networks like CNBC, CNN, and Bloomberg before striking out on her own to write a *New York Times* best-selling book called *Rich Bitch* about getting your financial life in order. Her book is fantastic, and—man or woman—if you've always had money or finance issues, you should definitely pick it up and read it cover to cover.

But what struck me about Nicole when we met was the story of her path to financial reporting that began, remarkably, at age 18. It was a journey that was almost over before it began, thanks to a whole different brand of adversity—the internal kind.

A first-generation American, Nicole grew up with immigrant parents who operated a 100 percent cash household. No credit cards, no loans, nothing that typically defined the average American's relationship with money. It was all cash, all the time.

"We didn't have the *Wall Street Journal* on the kitchen counter, we never talked about stocks or bonds or any of that, and I never learned it in school. So I was pretty clueless growing up," Nicole told me. "I was that awkward girl with no debit card who went out to dinner with girlfriends and either dropped a wad of cash or wrote a check."

The final straw came when she was in college at Northwestern University in Chicago and she needed to buy a last-minute airline ticket. The convenient thing would have been to hop on the computer and buy one online. There was just one problem: She didn't possess a credit card. Instead, she had to go to the bank, withdraw cash, and roll up to the counter at the airport and pay for the ticket with a wad of bills. "I said, 'Enough is enough. This is ridiculous.' I needed to take control of my life and my finances."

Except how do you do that? How do you take control of your financial life and set yourself on a path toward a career in business news when finance is essentially a foreign concept to you? When you can't learn from your parents? When you live in a country where they don't teach you how to master and manage your money—not in elementary school or high school or college, even if you take finance classes?

"That's when I realized, it's just a language, like anything else that's new. It's a very foreign language," Nicole said.

She was totally right! Every single new thing we attempt in our lives is like a new language. The language of MMA and mountain climbing probably scared the crap out of Kyle when he first thought about tackling those feats. The language of LinkedIn and the language of business scared me half to death when I was planted on my sister's couch staring at the end of my career in sports (a language I was very fluent in).

Getting started is always the hardest part of doing anything new. You have to overcome all those fears and anxieties of saying the wrong thing or looking foolish. There can be a lot of shame involved, and shame has stopped more than a few people from doing important things—things they loved. Nicole recognized this and decided to jump in with both feet. She took a job on the floor of the Chicago Mercantile Exchange.

"When you start to speak that language, you feel you're speaking Chinese in your own country," she confessed. "That's what happened to me when I started on the floor of the exchange. I had to learn the language really quickly. When I realized that it was just learning a language and that if I learned it I could join the conversation, I felt so empowered."

I knew exactly what she meant, because I experienced that exact feeling when I was learning how to salsa dance back in 2006. I was living above a jazz club that offered salsa dancing once a week, and I went down there committed to becoming the best tall, goofy, white-guy salsa dancer that I could be. I was petrified, but for 3 months, I trained and studied and had group classes, and I took private lessons, and I watched YouTube videos, and I practiced in front of my mirror by myself like I was dancing with a girl. If you think it's weird when I talk about it, imagine how weird I felt doing it!

But I remember the moment when I finally understood the language of salsa dancing, and believe me when I tell you that when I started, it seemed like a *completely* foreign language. Nicole nailed it; it was absolutely like speaking Chinese. When it clicked and salsa started to make sense, as though I could speak the language fluently, I felt like I could run up the side of a building. I could do anything I set my mind to no matter what obstacles—physical or mental, internal or external—stood in front of me.

Nicole helped me reframe my outlook on adversity—not just what it is and where it comes from but also how to address and overcome it. It's a lesson I will carry with me into every new challenge, because if there is one thing that is inescapable in life, to say nothing of the path to greatness, it is adversity. We dream, and then reality smacks us in the face. We create a vision for ourselves, and soon enough we learn that the world is, at best, indifferent to it (and us). In some cases, the world seems to want to do everything it can to get in our way. It shows up at nearly every stage along our path: from the early days of figuring out how to walk; learning in school; messing up your first kiss; practicing sports; starting a new business. We experience loads of pain, frustration, and falling down.

No one understands this better than Kyle Maynard. He taught me that not only is no one immune to adversity but that enduring your fair share of it is not an entirely bad thing. When we fail over and over in pursuit of excellence, it actually helps us learn and grow into greatness! Granted, Kyle has endured more than his fair share, compared to someone like me—I don't have a congenital disability, after all—but I still had obstacles to overcome.

THE HIDDEN ADVANTAGE OF ADVERSITY

My entire childhood was based around a singular vision: Become an All-American athlete. I thought it would be in football, the sport I'd lived and breathed for so many years. I thought it would happen my sophomore year in

college when I set the record for most receiving yards in
one game (418 yards) and ended the season with the second most receiving yards in the nation. But my team had
barely a .500 winning percentage, and they don't typically award All-American status to players on average
teams. Things only got worse from there, on and off the
field, as our coaching staff was unable to do what it took
to put us in a position to be great. So my senior season, I
transferred to another school that offered a real opportunity to achieve my dream. It was a tough decision to
leave, especially for someone like me who'd spent his
whole life playing with and for the team, but this new
school showed a lot of promise, and I couldn't deny the
dream that had guided my whole life.

In the second game of the season with my new team,
we were playing our crosstown rivals. I was having a
good game, making plays, and at one point in the third
quarter, I hauled in a slant pass over the middle and took
a hard hit to my ribs from one of the linebackers. I felt
some soreness at the time, but thanks to adrenaline and
competitiveness, I didn't think much of it. Then 2 days
later at practice, I went to make a quick cut in warmups,
heard a huge pop, and crumpled to the ground in absolute
agony. I'd never experienced that kind of pain in my life. It
felt like someone was stabbing me in the side, twisting
the knife, and then using a sledgehammer to pound on
the wound. My teammates thought I was joking because
nobody had touched me! Well, it turned out that I'd probably hairline fractured three ribs on my right side in the
game, and the quick cut and turn in practice did the rest

of the work, breaking them all the way. The cartilage had ripped from the bone and my muscles were twitching at the spot of the tear, chattering my ribs at the place of the breaks. I'd turned my rib cage into a wind chime, and every breath fluttered the chimes even more. Needless to say, I was out the rest of the season.

For a few months, I was in so much pain, I could hardly walk. I couldn't sleep, cough, sneeze, or laugh for at least 2 weeks. I had to have someone lift me out of bed because I couldn't engage my stomach muscles without needing to scream in pain. I had never taken pain medication before, so when I popped the pills the doctors prescribed, my body didn't know how to react to them and I threw them up almost immediately—which was a whole other level of pain to add to the mix.

Yet the physical pain paled in comparison to the emotional agony. I was completely crushed. My dream was slipping away—adversity had smashed my vision to pieces like that linebacker had smashed my ribs. It was one of the lowest points of my life.

Around Christmastime of that year, a few months after the injury occurred, I had recovered enough that I was able to run on a treadmill without pain. I was feeling a little better emotionally, too, but I still couldn't shake the fact that I was nowhere nearer to the goal that meant so much to me. I was a senior, and the football season was over, so becoming an All-American wide receiver was clearly no longer an option. I had to figure something out. There had to be another way.

That's when it occurred to me that I might try my

hand at another sport in the months remaining of my NCAA eligibility. Except for my still-healing ribs, I was in good shape, and I was a great track athlete. My freshman year, I jumped 6 feet 6 inches in the high jump and 22 feet in the long jump, and I'd nearly cracked 11 seconds in the 100-meter dash. None of those marks individually would get me within sniffing distance of a medal stand, let alone qualifying for the national championships, but together maybe there was something there. Track and field is a spring sport, so I called my old track coach (who had qualified for the Olympic trials and was a former All-American herself) between Christmas and New Year's and asked her what it would take to become an All-American in the decathlon—the 2-day, 10-event test of strength, agility, and endurance whose winner in the Olympics is often called the "world's greatest athlete." Was it even possible? She said it was, but training would have to start right away, and I would need to do everything she said for the next 6 grueling months. No shortcuts. No excuses.

To use Nicole Lapin's metaphor, it was a new language, but I didn't care—I was in. This new vision gave me the motivation and drive to refocus all of my energy toward doing whatever it took to make that happen. It brought a sense of purpose when before I felt helpless. It gave me that pep in my step that, just a few months prior on the football field, allowed me to distinguish myself as a top-flight wide receiver. I felt like a warrior preparing for battle again. A powerful vision gives us warrior-like strength, which is why it's critically important to find or recalibrate your vision as soon as possible after confronting major adversity.

I immediately began the arduous transfer process back to my previous school (Principia College, where my old track coach was based) and got to work. In the 6 months that followed, I ended up getting into the best shape of my life—probably my peak conditioning as an athlete to date—and not only qualifying for the national championships but making the All-American team. (I'll explain what happened in the next chapter.) Then, if that wasn't enough, I earned a fifth year of eligibility thanks to all the injuries, got back on the football field better than ever thanks to the decathlon training, broke a few receiving records and made big plays in big games, and earned my second All-American honors. This time— finally—in football, my goal all along.

I had unearthed the advantage hidden within my adverse circumstances. What I had dreaded and fought so hard against at first—my injuries—actually got me closer to my dream. In fact, it surpassed the original dream in ways I could have never imagined. How could that be? How could an injury, one that I never anticipated, literally double my chances to be an All-American, which I'd dreamed of since I was a boy?

I didn't realize it then, but it all became clear when I spoke to Ryan Holiday, my friend and author of the book *The Obstacle Is the Way*. Ryan is a best-selling author, the former head of marketing for American Apparel, and the founder of a marketing and strategy firm that allows him to live the life he wants to live. Ryan has faced his own fair share of adversity. He dropped out of college at 19 years old; was virtually disowned by his parents; went to work for a string of high-profile, very difficult, and controversial clients; and spent the better part of the next decade working his butt off to get where he is today.

"It is a timeless truth of history and philosophy," he told me, "that the hardships we face in life can be seen as terrible tragedies or opportunities." The Roman emperor Marcus Aurelius, one of Ryan's great influences, was fond of reminding himself that "the impediment to action advances action. What stands in the way becomes the way."

In fact, you can trace this foundational element of Stoic thought through many of the most revered individuals who ever lived. As young men, both Thomas Jefferson and George Washington read the Stoics—thinkers and leaders like Cato the Younger, Epictetus, and Marcus Aurelius—and it helped them with the adversity they faced during the creation of America. The explorer and writer Robert Louis Stevenson was a longtime admirer of Marcus Aurelius and Stoic thought. So were painters like Eugène Delacroix, writers and thinkers like Adam Smith, and statesmen like Bill Clinton. Tim Ferriss, the investor and entrepreneur and my personal friend, is also a public proponent of this line of ancient philosophy that has relevance for our modern lives.

All these folks faced adversity on their paths to success. Sometimes it was big; sometimes it was quite small.

As Ryan writes, there is "one thing that all great men and women have in common. Like oxygen to a fire, obstacles became fuel for that which was their ambition. Nothing could stop them, they were (and continue to be) impossible to discourage or contain. Every impediment served to make the inferno within them burn with greater ferocity."

YOUR PERSPECTIVE IS YOUR CHOICE

Kyle Maynard is a Stoic, too, whether he knows it or not. When he says, "Our perspective is always our choice," he is echoing what the philosophers have always claimed— that there is no good or bad but only our perceptions. As he tackled each of his dreams, undaunted, it was the philosopher-statesman Seneca's words that he took most vividly to heart: "It is a rough road that leads to the heights of greatness."

When Kyle started wrestling in high school, he recounted to me, "People would say, 'You'll never be able to win a match.' They wouldn't say it directly to me necessarily, but I'd hear it through the grapevine." A lot of that doubt came from people whose perceptions blinded them. They did not see the hungry dreamer in front of them, only what was missing from him. They saw only what limited him and held him back—not that it might have made him stronger or more determined or that it might have some tactical advantages on the mat!

Some of the doubt and negativity almost certainly came from a place of fear and insecurity that existed in the minds of his potential opponents. What if this armless, legless teenager beat them? How would *that* look? They were right to be afraid. Kyle not only won 36 matches his senior season but also finished 12th in his weight class at Senior Nationals, beating several state champions and higher-ranked wrestlers along the way.

Kyle used these fearful people's misperceptions and misunderstandings to his advantage. He found fuel in the haters. As Ralph Waldo Emerson asked, "Is it so bad, then, to be misunderstood? Pythagoras was misunderstood, and Socrates, and Jesus, and Luther, and Copernicus, and Galileo, and Newton, and every pure and wise spirit that ever took flesh. To be great is to be misunderstood." Obviously, I'm not trying to say that Kyle is on the same level as Socrates or Jesus or Galileo, but when it comes to guys who fought some uphill battles, you can find worse comparisons. Part of greatness is being doubted and facing difficulty, and it's precisely that struggle that contributes to their greatness.

A year later, Kyle decided he would try his hand at mixed martial arts and began the rigorous training. "MMA actually taught me a lot about myself," he said. "It was the first time that other people really voiced major disapproval with what I was doing." The State of Georgia attempted to ban his first match. The Georgia Athletic Commission refused to issue him a fighter's license—a prerequisite to compete in a sanctioned bout. The nay-saying grapevine from his wrestling days moved online, and they had no problem telling him exactly what they thought. Internet commenters were ruthless and relentless as they wrote about him in all of the major

MMA chat rooms and communities online. They threatened him; they called him a legless freak.

"One of my core beliefs is that you have to have things that you're passionate about to go after and live to your potential," Kyle said to me. "I didn't want to be a pro fighter. I had no delusions about that. I just wanted to experience it. Because 99.9 percent of the fans of the sport would never step into the cage, and that's okay, but I didn't want to be afraid. I wanted to go in there and experience it."

The great ones look at every situation this way. They look at adversity as the lesson that moves them toward their goal, not the obstacle that keeps them from it. Fear drove Kyle's opponents and haters to lash out at him. It also drove them off the mat and out of the cage. It drove Kyle to test his limits and pursue his dreams with even more energy and purpose. As the great Lionel Richie put it, "Greatness comes from fear. Fear can either shut us down and we go home, or we fight through it."

This is why adversity is so important and why it is the second lesson in this book. First we have our vision, and then we run into obstacles. The real greats don't worry too much about this—it's inevitable, it's not the end of the world. Instead, this dose of reality is simply used as a challenge. To learn a new language. To channel their energy into their true path. To adjust their vision from fantasy into an actionable, realistic plan.

It occurred to me that this was the common thread in Kyle's life, as he repeatedly said to himself: "Okay, what is it that I should not able to do, and how can I do it? How can I figure out a way to do it?" It applied to tackling a ball carrier in his adolescent years, to speaking among giants in his late teens, and to climbing Kilimanjaro in his twenties. He was born without arms and legs, so he's simply had to modify and adjust and be adaptive to everything, to everyday life.

In this way, we must be grateful for our particular form of adversity, since it is the precise thing that helps us get to where we want to be. *What stands in the way becomes the way.* For instance, I was shocked to hear that not only does Kyle spend a lot of time working with veterans who've lost limbs in war, but when he meets them, he feels a kind of gratitude. Not reluctance or kinship or pity, but gratitude.

"I don't have any idea what it's like to lose my limbs. I was born without my arms and legs, so I have no perspective of that," he said. This is how it's always been for him. He was spared the enormous sense of loss and fear that these veterans feel. He was spared their pain, too, and the lingering effects of injury. Just think about the perspective it takes to live with that kind of attitude—to be grateful for something like being born with a disability because there are worse ways to end up where you are. That perspective and attitude inspire me. Whenever I seem to be having a "bad day," I think about Kyle and realize how much I have to be grateful for as well.

This is something that great men and women understand—that the actual problem, obstacle, or adversity is irrelevant. It's their mindset and response to it that matter. They learn from these obstacles what it is going to take to accomplish what they've set out to do. They learn the importance of persevering toward their vision *despite* that adversity. They learn the language so they can tell the world what they want to do and who they want to become.

It's funny, when I was speaking with Angel Martinez, this came up almost verbatim. Like me, Angel ultimately became successful in business (way bigger than me, obviously!) through a combination of vision, talent, and perseverance, and he discovered early on that the path to self-esteem was sweaty and intense and competitive— and not where he first expected to find it. I thought I would find it on the receiving end of touchdown passes. It turns out it was at the end of 10 grueling track-and-field events. Angel thought it would be baseball.

"I wanted to play Major League Baseball, like every Cuban kid, but when I was a freshman in high school, I think I was about 5 foot 3 inches and 112 pounds. I couldn't hit or throw the ball out of the infield. I could field well, but that was about it. I could throw to first and second. That was okay when we were playing Little League, but when we got to high school, it was a whole other thing," he told me.

Like Kyle and me, one of Angel's childhood dreams ran smack into the unforgiving reality of physical limitations. And like us, he had to find a way around them. For Angel, it was running.

"What attracted me to running was that I could be as good as I wanted to be," he said. "In distance running, there's no coach who is going to bench you or tell you that you can't play. And the clock never lies. There's no subjectivity. I remember when I started running, the older guys on the team told me, 'We only have one rule. You can't stop. You can go as slow as you need to go, but you cannot stop. You can never drop out.' "

SLOW AND STEADY WINS A DIFFERENT RACE

If there is one thing you take from the School of Greatness about pursuing your vision and achieving your dreams, it should be this: You can go as slow as you need to go, but you cannot stop. You can never give up or drop out of giving your best in your life.

Angel unwittingly taught his own son Julian, a cross-country runner at Claremont McKenna College, this lesson. "He had always heard me talk about all this," Angel said of Julian. "Then I went to watch him at one meet, and he was about halfway through the 5 miles when he felt a really sharp pain in his shin area. He started slowing down, and I could see something was wrong. I went out there and said, 'Julian, what's the matter?' He was grimacing but he ignored me, and he finished the race." It turns out, Julian had broken his leg at the 2.5-mile mark. Two hours after the finish, he was in a cast. When Angel asked him why he didn't stop, Julian's answer was simple and obvious: "I don't drop out, Dad." Make no mistake, true greats never drop out.

Of course, you don't want to put yourself through any type of trauma or pain intentionally that will hurt you in the long run (more on the importance of experiencing pain in Chapter 5), but it is the idea and intention behind not giving up or dropping out on giving your best effort at all times. That is what we are talking about here.

"The lesson of running is about what it takes to be successful in life," Angel told me. "It is a metaphor for a lot of things you need to learn. Running, like life, is that constant confrontation of a challenge every day. Some days you don't feel that good; some days you feel great. Some days you're not inspired; other days it's pouring rain and freezing cold but you still have to go and run. As a kid, that's an incredibly important lesson to learn: that it takes commitment and you have to believe in yourself and that you can actually do whatever the hell you want. There's no limit to what you can do."

I discovered the same thing during my decathlon training, and I am reaping the benefits to this day as I train with the United States men's national handball team. There have been many moments when I didn't feel like training, especially after an injury. I've experienced many injuries over the past 4 years as I've trained for this new sport. I pulled my groin three times; I stuck a needle in my elbow multiple times to drain fluid; I've sprained ankles, broken fingers, and even took an elbow to the throat that had me spitting up blood for a week. The list of bumps, breaks, and bruises feels almost endless. But each injury taught me a lesson, and after each recovery, I took the necessary steps to keep moving and (hopefully) learn from them and use them to my advantage going forward. Once you experience the power of this triumph over adversity—over *yourself* in many ways—it's enough to get you off the couch and back into the game. Kyle Maynard experienced it, too. He has experienced it every day of his life. But it doesn't just get him off the couch, it puts him on the side of mountains in the middle of Africa.

Kyle ascended Tanzania's 19,336-foot Mount Kilimanjaro as part of a nine-man team in early 2012. Unassisted by team members and unaided by prosthetics, he essentially bear-crawled on his elbows for $12^1/_2$ days—10 days up, $2^1/_2$ days down. Half a dozen people (with all their limbs) die on that mountain every year. To summit it at all is a serious achievement. To do it like Kyle did it, well, I don't think there is even a word for that except for *greatness*!

Kyle would disagree, obviously, because that is not how he perceives his situation. In fact, the truly striking thing is that the climb wasn't about him at all. Born in a US Army hospital to an Army dad, Kyle has always had a passion for working with veterans. This mission up Kilimanjaro was for them. The goal, he told me, was "just to send a message to some of our troops that have literally sacrificed their limbs for our freedom that 'You may have had this happen to you, but you're still able to go and create the life that you want. It may not include climbing Kilimanjaro, but you have something that you want to do.'"

At some point, adversity happens in everyone's life. It usually comes unannounced, and it doesn't arrive with flowers and candy. It takes different forms and hits each of us differently, but learning to address and overcome it is all about bending but not breaking in the face of the daunting situations it presents. It requires connecting your head and your heart to that deep well of energy within to push you forward in a positive direction.

Kyle had to do it 4 days into his trek up Kilimanjaro as his elbows and feet swelled in incredible pain and nearly broke him. Angel Martinez did it as a runner, struggling to push himself through every mile. The problem he faced, as he tried to run faster and farther, was that the shoes his team wore weren't very good. To get halfway decent running shoes, they'd have to go into Berkeley (he eventually had moved from the Bronx to the Bay Area) and buy shoes that had been imported by a company called Blue Ribbon Sports. The importer? His name was Phil Knight, and he went on to found Nike.

Angel saw these people making a living solving a problem in the sport he loved and thought: *Why not me? Why can't I make a living by connecting my current passion [running] with one of my earliest childhood passions [cool shoes]?* Eventually, he started working at a small shop and bought half of it from the owner. A few years later, a couple of English guys walked in with a new brand they hoped he would sell. They called it Reebok.

This is what I mean when I say that the obstacle can be the way. If he hadn't been too short, if he hadn't felt like he had something to prove, Angel never would have found himself exposed to the business that changed his life—that became his calling. As Angel puts it, "There's always a challenge if you don't see yourself as a conventional person," so you'd better be prepared and ready for adversity—ready to make the most of it.

Whenever shit would hit the fan for me over the last couple years, I somehow automatically come back to Kyle and Angel and think, *Gosh, how could I possibly have anything to be ungrateful for?* Sure, like anyone, I have things I can be unhappy about. I am not talking about being a Pollyanna or staring at life through rose-colored glasses. This isn't self-delusion. What I am talking about is looking at things with your eyes open. When I was younger, I would get down on myself if something bad happened or get depressed if I felt things weren't going my way. Now I remember, in a way that is real and meaningful, that I have miraculous advantages that many others have not had. If Kyle can accomplish all that he has, if Angel can go from a Bronx tenement to the corner office of a billion-dollar business, I can pursue my own dreams and strive for my own version of greatness without giving in to a bad attitude when things invariably don't go my way. Whenever I face adversity, I'm always reminded of the examples they set, and I am thankful for our friendship every day because of it.

When you're looking at things with your eyes open, with a different perspective, it is then that you truly see the opportunities at your doorstep and how you can use them to your advantage. At the end of the day, if achieving dreams was easy, then everyone would have done it and no one would suffer from that nagging feeling that either drives or depresses us. What makes achieving your dreams and fulfilling your vision that much more special is the hard work it takes to get there. Proving that adversity is no match for you. That's what this is all about!

EXERCISE:
Embrace the Adversity (Internal and External)

Adversity is difficulty or misfortune that, for most people, creates an unmanageable amount of stress. Those who learn how to use adversity to their advantage, however, possess the power to turn that adversity into greatness. This is easier said than done, of course, because no one actually *likes* adversity. When you first experience it and you aren't prepared, what it feels like is failure. Adversity means failure, and failure means you must be bad at something. That's an awful feeling.

In reality, failure is simply feedback. It's not that you are bad or not good enough or incapable. Failure (or feedback) gives you the opportunity to look at what's not working and figure out how to make it work.

Everyone fails. Highly successful people fail many more times than the rest of the world and with much higher stakes at hand. Once we understand this, we can look at failure as something to fall in love with instead of something to shy away from. Thomas Edison endured 10,000 failures before he made the lightbulb, but each "failure" was feedback telling him that he hadn't figured it out yet and that this particular set of choices wasn't the right one for this particular task. His failures weren't evidence of his incompetence—if anything, they highlighted his brilliance and increased the likelihood that the next attempt would be the successful one.

Oftentimes the biggest obstacle we face is ourselves. Negative feelings, self-doubt, self-loathing; they all come from within to sabotage our vision. Adversity of all kinds will remain in your life until you adjust your perspective and embrace the messages failure is trying to send you. Listen to the feedback and apply it to your actions, and before you know it, adversity begins to melt away.

This is an exercise you can and should practice when those negative feelings threaten to overwhelm you. Consider it a daily practice until you fully start shifting and living consistently in a positive way that will support you and your vision instead of bring you down.

Step 1: Be Aware of the Adversity

Adversity happens to everyone, and though pain is inevitable, despair is optional. Discover precisely what the adversity is and why it is happening. This is your opportunity to take responsibility for every type of adversity that comes your way. Focus on the *why*—the root of it.

There are two types of adversity.

1. **The minor daily adversities that come up from time to time:** Fighting in your relationship, not getting the raise you want at your job, getting parking tickets, receiving poor grades on homework, feeling exhausted and stressed, feeling unsafe in your environment, etc.

2. **The major singular adversities that are more rare:** A death in the family, a car crash, injury or illness, a major breakup, losing your job, going bankrupt, etc.

When you become aware that adversity is inevitable, it allows you to prepare for it happening in the future.

What adversities do you face right now? What in your life feels like it is standing in the way of fulfilling your vision and achieving greatness?

Write your adversities down. Then identify whether they are chronic, daily obstacles that seem to grind your progress to a halt or big, singular moments of struggle that have thrown you off the path.

How have you been dealing with these issues to this point? How have you dealt with similar issues in the past? Have you overcome any of them? What did you do? There is wisdom and insight to be gleaned from your answers to those questions if not about what to do, then definitely about what *not* to do.

If you're anything like many of my coaching clients and some of the great teachers you will meet in the coming chapters, the thing you did most often in the face of adversity when you were first starting out was either try to ignore it or avoid it. Sometimes you might even pretend it wasn't there. I know I've been guilty of each of those behaviors in my own past.

Needless to say, this is something you absolutely cannot do. You cannot avoid, ignore, or deny adversity. Be aware of which adversities you are facing and accept the adversity for what it is. Avoid it or resist it and it will only persist.

Step 2: Write It Down or Share It

Now that you are aware of the adversity, write down how it's making you feel and why you think it's making you feel that way. This helps let go of the stress you are feeling to a certain degree and gets it out of you, where it can be the most toxic and do the most damage. It also allows you to have a written record of what you are feeling over time so you can look for patterns and see areas of growth. Write it down with pen and paper. If you don't have that, put it in your phone or on your computer. Over time, you'll want this all in one place so you can refer to it, so keep that in mind. Get it out! Embrace it.

For example: I'm angry/stressed/frustrated because I had an argument with my girlfriend; upset that I lost my job; still shaking after I got in a car crash, etc.

If you hold this inside, it will only bring more adversity to your life. Remember, what you resist persists.

If you prefer to verbally express yourself, then find a dedicated "adversity friend" whom you can go to anytime you feel frustrated by failure or you're struggling through adversity. Make an agreement with this friend that is reciprocal—you'll always listen to them without judgment so they can purge their emotions, and they will be your sounding board in return.

In the next chapter, you'll read stories and go through exercises that will support you in finding resolution in these breakdowns.

Step 3: Acknowledge Yourself

Once you let the negative feeling go, replace it by acknowledging yourself for all that you have done that day/week/month/year. You are up to big things! Even if they seem small to you, they are always bigger than where you were earlier in your life. Most of the time, we are comparing ourselves to others in our family or careers, and we do more harm by comparing ourselves rather than giving ourselves credit for where we are along our journey. Acknowledge yourself for reading this—knowledge is power. Your good intention is there.

Examples of things you can acknowledge yourself for: being on time at work, consistently going to the gym or working out, eating clean, being your word, etc.

Step 4: Express Your Gratitude

It's hard to be upset when you are focusing on what you are grateful for. Verbally tell your significant other, a friend, a family member, or just someone around you three things you are most grateful for in this moment; then ask them what three things they are most grateful for in their lives. Obviously, you don't have to tell the other people that you are beating yourself up on the inside right now, but just be aware in the moment and shift into a conversation of gratitude. When you give, you automatically receive. It's amazing what a compliment to someone opens up.

Examples: I'm grateful for my amazing friends. I'm grateful for my health and that I can walk, see, and feel. I'm grateful for my family and the support they give me. I'm grateful for the bed I get to sleep on.

Step 5: Reconnect to Your Vision and Take Action

Return your focus to what you want to achieve and why you want to achieve it: your Certificate of Achievement and your Personal Statement Plan from Chapter 1. Then figure out the next step to making your vision happen, and take action toward it. Momentum helps build confidence and positive thoughts and feelings, so it's important to spring into action when you are down on yourself or feeling adversity.

Whenever you are in breakdown or battling adversity in any situation in your life, this five-step process will help you fight off the insidious nature of self-defeating negative thoughts and chart a positive path toward achieving your vision and becoming great.

COACHING TIP

Learn to fall in love with adversity. Don't fall into a victim mindset and look at it as the thing that is holding you back, but instead find the part of it that can launch you toward achieving your dreams. Remember, no one has ever achieved anything truly great without going through extreme adversity. That doesn't mean you have to suffer through every challenge. Balance out the difficulties that adversity brings by being grateful for what is good in your life and treat yourself with gentle care. Give yourself time to heal, be messy, and experience the painful feelings you are battling. It's okay. You are human. Beating yourself up during adversity is the worst thing you can do, so make sure to love yourself and surround yourself with those who support you and lift you up. Tune back in to your vision, your Certificate of Achievement, and the principles you stand for. Once you are ready, take the next step toward your dreams and living that perfect day. It's within your reach; you are closer and closer to bringing it to reality. Accept and embrace adversity. Failure is simply feedback. Use it and stay committed to your vision through taking action at all times. Don't stop now. Keep moving forward. You've got this, and I've got your back.

GET GROUNDED

There is a big difference between the person who gets great results and the person who gets average results. And it begins with the conversations in the space between their ears—with how they believe in themselves. When you start to believe in the gifts you have within you, you are already halfway to becoming great. To do this, you must accept where you currently are along your journey and understand that if you are not happy, you have the power to change it. All you have to do is learn the necessary skills and put in the work.

This chapter is about teaching you the skills necessary to develop such a powerful belief in yourself that your mindset won't be shaken even under the most extreme challenges. Take notes and prepare to equip yourself with a powerful inner voice and a deeper understanding of what it takes to become a champion. This isn't just a lesson for sports; it applies equally to life, love, business, and spirit.

CHAPTER 3

CULTIVATE A CHAMPION'S MINDSET

I understand that nothing is easy.
I say everything happens for a reason.
I dream of one day the world is in peace.
I try to see the good in everything,
I'm a caring girl who loves to flip.

—Shawn Johnson, seventh grade

Michael Jordan, Serena Williams, Michael Phelps, Tom Brady, Janet Evans, Michael Johnson, Mia Hamm, Michael Schumacher (that's a lot of Michaels, but you get the idea). What is it like inside the minds of these champions and champions like them? From a distance, they appear superhuman or super lucky or both. They get all the calls, all the money, all the best parking spots. The ball always seems to bounce their way.

It's like they are living in a different world than the rest of us, and in a way they are. Their world is crystal clear. It isn't foggy and tumultuous and filled with self-doubt, like ours can be if we haven't clarified our vision, battled through adversity, and developed the proper mindset—the champion's mindset.

The champion's mindset is all about focus, flow, belief, and emotional intelligence. It is the complete dedication to your vision of future achievement. The way I have learned to describe it to myself when I do the visualization exercise you will learn at the end of this chapter is as a unique headspace that allows you to focus all your energy on putting yourself in the best position physically, mentally, and emotionally to be successful.

Don't misunderstand when I say the headspace is unique. I don't mean that only some people are capable of having it. I mean that the vision for greatness that defines your mindset and drives your effort is unique to you. I also mean that it is a mindset different than any other you will experience in your life.

I've tasted what it's like inside the mind of a champion. In fact, most of us probably have—we just didn't know it at the time. I didn't realize it the first time it happened to me; I just thought I was doing what needed to be done. I was simply focusing on the task in front of me, completely and totally. It turns out, that is a major component in the mind of a champion, and I learned it on the end of a 15-foot pole and a 40-meter runway.

It was the early summer of my senior year in college. I'd just spent the last 6 months stretching, pushing, pulling, lifting, and willing myself into the best shape of my life in preparation for the NCAA Division III track-and-field national championships in Waverly, Iowa. Held over 2 days, my event, the decathlon, would put all my hard work to the test. After breaking three ribs in the second football game of the season less than a year before, I had come back stronger than ever. I thought the injury had permanently derailed my dream of becoming an All-American, but the decathlon had breathed new life into the dying dream, and if I finished among the top eight competitors, that dream would become a reality.

When the competition began, I was pumped with adrenaline and feeling strong. On the first day of the 2-day event, I did well in some events and not so well in others. I entered the second day of competition right around ninth place, and I knew that I had to excel in the third event of the day, the pole vault, in order to reach the All-American podium.

In the pole vault, each competitor has to clear an opening height to score points. You get three attempts at each height after that, but if you fail to clear the initial height, you get a zero score for that event (which would essentially eliminate you from placing in the top of the competition). On my first attempt at the national championships, I opened at a height I cleared comfortably in practice: 12 feet. I was confident in my approach, ran down the runway, and leaped so high over the bar that I could have cleared 15 feet, but I ended up grazing the bar on the way down and watched it roll off the stands. No worries, though; I still had two attempts left and knew I'd make it on the next one. On my second attempt, I tried to run harder than before and in the process overstretched my footing and missed my mark. I stopped running about 2 feet ahead of my ideal takeoff spot and tried to compensate by lunging forward. I went straight up 15 feet in the air and fell straight back down on the runway, missing the bar completely. Suddenly, the third—and last—attempt took on unexpected weight and pressure. I was only 22 years old, but I felt like my entire life had come down to this moment. Make it and I have a shot at being an All-American. Miss it and my entire 22 years, along with the grueling 6 months of training to prepare for this moment, would be for nothing. That's how I felt. My dream of greatness came down to this.

The pole vault is all about strength, technique, and timing. For a decathlete, it is often a make-or-break event. In 1992, Angel Martinez's old company, Reebok, ran a giant advertising campaign in the lead-up to the Summer Olympics in Barcelona centered around American decathletes Dan O'Brien and Dave Johnson, called "Dan & Dave." They were two of the best decathletes in the world and favored to win medals. There was only one problem: Dan didn't qualify for the Olympics at the Trials. Want to guess why? He no-heighted on the pole vault, missing all three attempts. "Dan & Dave" became "Dave . . . and all those other guys."

My coach looked at me with a calm confidence through her piercing eyes, and strangely, instead of panicking, I began to visualize back to when I was 6 or 7 years old, sitting on the couch with my dad, watching football together and his explaining to me about the All-Americans we were seeing and what it meant to become one of them. The sense of honor and purpose, above the athletic achievements, stuck with me. It cleared away my current confusion and distractions. It lifted the lead weight from my feet. I was aware not only of exactly what I had to do but also of exactly who I was and what I was capable of. That moment put me into intense focus as I sprinted down the track with the pole, hitting my mark and launching myself over the bar with ease. Relief and joy hit me simultaneously. I went on to make a personal best, clearing over 14 feet, that day in the pole vault, and I finished strong in the next two events.

I became an All-American that day.

I have felt versions of that laser focus a handful of times over the past decade in many areas of my life besides sports, including business and relationships. It's addictive. Yet some of us have never felt it—we may not know that it is absent and what feats we're missing out on because of it. Some of us haven't even come close to feeling that state of peak performance and excellence.

I never performed remotely close to my best before that day in the pole vault. That isn't to say I didn't do well other times, but the difference between being good and being fully in the zone—truly in the head space of a champion—is a crucial ingredient in greatness, whether we're talking about sports, business, or life. And it was that day, lying on the vault mat, looking up at the bar still in its blocks 12 feet above my head, that I realized the power of accessing the zone for all areas of your life. I am calling it "laser focus" now, but I didn't fully recognize what I'd been channeling in that moment until I spoke with two amazing people: Steven Kotler and US Olympic gymnast Shawn Johnson—both fully tenured professors of greatness as far as I'm concerned.

Steven Kotler is the author of *The Rise of Superman: Decoding the Science of Ultimate Human Performance*. To say that his book is the one that I had been waiting for my whole life is legitimately an understatement. Growing up a skinny white kid in middle Ohio, all I ever wanted was to figure out what advantages I could get as an athlete to raise my game to the next level and perform at my peak in every sport. I wanted to know how to get in the zone like the All-Americans and world champions I admired—or, as Steven refers to it, the "flow state."

"Flow," Steven told me, "is an optimal state of consciousness, where we perform our best and we feel our best. In flow, we are so focused on the task at hand that everything else vanishes. Time either speeds up, so 5 hours will pass by like 5 minutes, or it slows down, like that freeze-frame effect in a car crash. Your sense of self, your sense of self-consciousness disappear completely, and all aspects of performance, mental and physical, go through the roof."

Yes! That is exactly how I felt as I sprinted down the runway on the track in Waverly, Iowa, drove the pole into the pit, and vaulted myself over the bar and closer to my dream. Talking with Steven, I realized I was wrong about one thing, though: This wasn't my first experience with flow. I'd had a similar experience on the football field as a sophomore 2 years earlier, in a game where I just felt invincible—unstoppable. It was my record-breaking game.

I remember in the first quarter they put one defensive back on me. Before I knew it, there were two on me and then there were three, with the safety shading over. Eventually, it felt like the whole team had been assigned to cover me, but it didn't matter how many people they put on my side of the field, what they did, or what they tried to do. The ball was still coming my way, and I was catching every one of them. I felt like one of the Green Bay Packers wide receivers in the Monday Night Football game against the Oakland Raiders in 2003 when Brett Favre played the day after his father died. They caught everything, no matter where he put the ball. That's what it was like.

The funny thing was, we actually lost the game by a touchdown (42–35), and I remember at the end of the game being more depressed than anything, feeling like I didn't catch enough balls or get enough yards. I had no clue what my stats were or what I had done, yet everyone was coming up to congratulate me as we were taking off our pads in the locker room. "Man, you had an unbelievable game. How many catches do you think you had?" I had no idea. I thought 8, 10 maybe, which was a good game for me or any wide receiver. But I didn't want to think about it. So finally I hit the showers, beating myself up, thinking, *What could I have done better? How could I have been a better teammate?* I was the last one out of the locker room, just wallowing in my own misery of this loss, and my coach came up to me and said, "I just wanted to say congratulations. You actually broke a world record for the most receiving yards in a single football game: 418 yards."

Four hundred eighteen yards on 17 catches, including four touchdowns, to be exact. Yup. I was in a flow state. The kind that champions live in and greatness results from. To be honest, I was a little in shock at that moment. I was happy to hear the news that I accomplished something that had never happened before in the history of collegiate football (or any level), but I also felt responsible for our loss and was preoccupied with figuring out how I could have done things better. It was a bittersweet moment, but one I'll always remember, not only because of the record but also because I felt like Superman in that flow state, and I knew I wanted to feel that way all of the time, on and off the field.

Fortunately, flow doesn't happen only for athletes, I learned from Steven. The consulting firm McKinsey did a 10-year study of top executives in flow. They found top executives in flow are five times more productive than when out of flow. That's 500 percent more productive. DARPA* did a study with snipers, inducing flow artificially using transcranial direct stimulation and teaching snipers target acquisition skills. The snipers learned the skills 230 percent faster. In a separate nonmilitary study, DARPA also induced flow artificially and cut the time it took to train a novice sniper up to an expert level by 50 percent.

So that's what flow is and what it does, but how do you get it? How do you achieve the kind of flow state that leads to 418-yard receiving games, 230 percent increases in learning, or 500 percent increases in productivity?

---

*DARPA is the acronym for the Defense Advanced Research Projects Agency. It is essentially the R&D division of the US Department of Defense. Lockheed Martin has its Skunk Works; the Defense Department has DARPA. Most famously, DARPA is responsible for the creation of the Internet.

"It's twofold," Steven explained. On the one hand, it happens "out of necessity. Meaning the level of performance has gone up so much that in the case of athletes, at least, if you are not in flow when you're performing, you're going to end up in the hospital or dead." I could definitely relate to that. With three guys covering me, if I go over the middle for a pass and I am not in flow, I am on the ground with the wind knocked out of me or with another case of cracked ribs.

The other reason it happens is because you've surrounded yourself with all the necessary flow triggers. True greats have basically created the most high-flow environment they possibly could. Everything in their lives is triggering flow. Psychologists talk about it as the source code of intrinsic motivation. Another way of putting it is that the five neurochemicals you get during flow—norepinephrine, dopamine, anandamide, serotonin, and endorphin—are the most addictive chemicals on earth. They make you quicker, faster, stronger, and more motivated. According to Steven, they do the same thing for your mental output that they do for your physical output.

Talk about an aha moment.

What Steven was saying is that flow is really all about mindset—how you perceive your situation and how you receive information. To be in flow, to sidestep adversity like it is nothing and vault yourself toward your vision, you need to have a champion's mindset.

There's a great quote by Bruce Lee in John Little's documentary *Bruce Lee: A Warrior's Journey* that explains flow, when he talks about becoming like water: "I said empty your mind. Be formless, shapeless. Like water. You put water into a cup, it becomes the cup. You put water into a bottle, it becomes the bottle. You put it in a teapot, it becomes the teapot. Now water can flow, or it can crash. Be water, my friend. Like that, you see." The champion's mindset, to me, is becoming like water.

Though I'd tasted it in my life and found confirmation of my feelings with Steven, it wasn't until I met my next teacher that I saw these ideas in the living, walking flesh. You'd be hard-pressed to find, pound for pound, someone with a more powerful champion's mindset in the world than Shawn Johnson. At 4 feet 9 inches and 90 pounds and just 16 years old, with hundreds of millions of people watching live and on television, she won an Olympic gold medal in the balance beam and three silver medals in the team, individual all-around, and floor exercise disciplines at the 2008 Beijing Olympic Games. Then, as if to prove her remarkable determination was no fluke, Shawn gave the country a seminar on how to translate the champion's mindset into other areas of life by winning season eight of *Dancing with the Stars* not long after she returned from Beijing.

From the moment I met Shawn, I knew she was the professor who could teach me how to cultivate the right mindset. I'm 6 foot 4 and she is a shade under 5 feet tall, so naturally we went and did a CrossFit workout together one day to see who could beat out the other in a battle of the fittest. This is my book, so I'm not going to say in print that she whipped my butt, but let's just say that she beat me (and the rest of the class) so badly that it was embarrassing. Not that it should be—this is a woman who has performed and won at the hardest level of sports, in front of billions of people, all before she was old enough to vote. Obviously she is physically gifted, but I think we would both agree that her triumph over me (oh, and the entire gymnastics world) had as much to do with the power of the right mindset as anything else.

"Gymnastics taught me everything—life lessons, responsibility, discipline, and respect," Shawn told me. Imagine the training and discipline she had to embrace at an age when the rest of us were playing video games and hoping for our first kiss. Imagine the focus and the clarity of purpose and the self-awareness it required. This is all part of the champion's mindset. For years, I tried to imagine it, but that part always seemed to be missing from my game. It was the part I could see in the greats and the athletes who practically lived in a flow state and to whom I'd always compared myself (all those Michaels). Yet I struggled with it, and continue to periodically, in life and business, even today.

The reason, I think, is because the champion's mindset is fundamentally about belief. If there's one thing I know about champions, it's that they all have a strong belief in something. Usually they believe they are the greatest thing in the world (like Muhammad Ali) or they believe they have been graced by the guiding hand of a higher power. All you have to do is listen to an athlete being interviewed after a big game to see this in action. The announcer says to them, "Congratulations on the win, you were amazing out there today! How did you do it?" And the player usually responds one of two ways: Either they say, "I want to give thanks to God for giving me these gifts and being by my side, as all the glory goes to him," or they grab the mike, look directly into the camera, and go on and on about how hard they trained and how no one can beat them and how they are the greatest competitor to ever walk this earth in their sport (think Floyd "Money" Mayweather Jr. in boxing). Regardless of the ego involved, it continues to be true that most of the *greatest* athletes have such a powerful belief in themselves and their desire to accomplish their goals that nothing can stand in their way. Not even failure. It's this 100 percent confidence that they will achieve what they want that is a difference maker on the path to greatness.

I have accomplished a lot of goals since my days in Ohio. I've achieved success, earned a lot of money, but for years it was driven by anger, ego, and resentment. That's what fueled my passion to be successful, and it resulted in a lot of ups and downs. There'd be big moments, and then there would be vast lows of hurt, pain, insecurity, frustration, and loneliness. It was because deep down I didn't believe in myself and wasn't sure if others believed in me, either. I had a clear vision, I had more than my fair share of adversity, but this lack of belief prevented me from creating the kind of champion's mindset that would make flow state more readily accessible and greatness inevitable.

Another amazing person in the School of Greatness, 27-year transformation coach and leadership expert Chris Lee, talked to me in depth about this very issue. "I believe that the most powerful work we can do with ourselves is develop the strategies to uncover, redesign, and reinvent our belief system," he said. "Because the only way you're going to have your business be successful, the only way you're going to have your relationships be successful, the only way you're going to have your life be successful, is by elevating who you are being. You bring that into what you're doing, and that affects what you have. Because if we keep repeating the same thing over and over, we're going to have the same result."

Chris highlighted an issue that many of us face in our pursuit of greatness. We keep doing the same thing, oftentimes blaming external factors for our dissatisfaction, instead of looking within at our beliefs—at our mindset. There is a flip side to a strong belief in self, however, and it is one of the most powerful lessons I learned from my conversations with Shawn Johnson. It was about humility. The champion cannot allow ego and confidence to devolve into self-delusion. Belief in yourself has to be a weapon in your arsenal whose power you respect and revere; it can't be used like impenetrable armor that creates a sense of invincibility or superiority. That distinction can be the difference between achieving your dreams and being blindsided by failure (or getting to the top, then falling quickly once you are there).

Shawn used her belief as a weapon on the balance beam in Beijing. "She takes command of the apparatus," the commentator said as she worked through her routine atop the 4-inch-wide beam 4 feet off the ground.

"You can see, she is in charge." She won gold because she was in charge of her belief in herself and therefore everything she encountered. This is not always the case for a lot of people.

"I've seen the type of belief in self that can be destructive," she told me. "Because if you are that person who says, 'I believe so strongly that I'm going to win, and I believe so strongly I've given my all,' you're not opening yourself up to be able to see and respond to what other people are doing in the actual competition. When that happens, it can become a cop-out when you run into adversity."

That is why an equally important part of the champion's mindset is the pursuit of perfection and excellence, independent of external results. This is very different from a drive to "win." Shawn, like many athletes, isn't obsessed with winning so much as she is with doing her absolute best: "I never focused on winning. Especially when I started out and I was in 30-something place out of 39 people. It was never about winning. I couldn't have cared less. I just always wanted to do better. I think the only thing that really made me want to work more and get on top of the podium was the feeling of pride you have when you're successful. It had nothing to do with a medal; that was just extra. It was knowing I had done my best and I was being acknowledged for it. It was about knowing at the end of the day that I worked as hard as I possibly could, and even if a score is worth the very last place, I couldn't be any happier."

Cultivating the mindset of a champion is not an overnight task. Vision, focus, discipline, belief in self, humility, and the pursuit of greatness are all the products of developed emotional intelligence—a fine art that requires a lot of practice. You never "arrive" at this point of knowing and having it all. Greatness is not something that is delivered to you or you are delivered to. It's something you have to work on daily. It takes years of dedication, discipline, and drive that persist in spite of any and all of the constant changes that inevitably occur with your health, business, relationships, and the world around you. If you commit to the process of developing this mindset for yourself, you will blow past every limit you thought was unbreakable.

Steven Kotler has shown us what flow is and why it happens. Shawn Johnson has given us the elements of the champion's mindset that are a prerequisite for flow and for greatness—foremost among them focus, dedication, and a belief in yourself that is tempered by humility. Chris Lee has implored us to reevaluate our personal belief system, the ideas and principles that undergird everything we are trying to do and become. Oftentimes it is those things that are impeding us on our journey toward greatness, not the external factors we love to blame when we run into adversity.

In fact, it wasn't until I had fully absorbed all these lessons that my podcast really started to take off. What most people don't know is that *The School of Greatness* podcast began as an extension of my online business; it did not start with a grand plan. Fortunately, it gathered a little bit of steam over the following couple of months, thanks to the network I'd built up on social media. Still, it wasn't really going anywhere that I could point to because I hadn't truly articulated a vision for it (I had for myself—I wanted to pick all these great teachers' brains—but that wasn't enough), so it was impossible to develop the kind of focus I needed. As a result, any adversity I faced felt like a mountain instead of a molehill. Beginning with my work with Chris Lee, I started to turn things around and really focus on doing shows that reflected my personal beliefs and helped as many people as possible. Being in a space that I was very comfortable with not only gave me confidence in myself but also tapped into the energy and desire I had previously felt only on the playing field. Then, before I knew it, the podcast started taking off and now here we are.

But you might be asking, "How do you do it? What is the process?" Like Shawn Johnson, thousands of champions have turned inward to develop these positive attributes. Through visualization, meditation, mindfulness, and a focus on cultivating emotional intelligence, they have learned to tap into a powerful belief that they can succeed; that their vision is clear, their obstacles are surmountable, and their path to greatness is a reality.

I've developed a number of great exercises to help you with each step in the process: visualization, meditation, mindfulness, and emotional intelligence. Do these and the building blocks of a champion's mindset will begin to stack themselves.

EXERCISE #1:
Visualization

The purpose of visualization is to see the results you want to create, before they happen. This is something I did in sports every season (and continue to do in life on a regular basis).

In football, I wanted to be a great wide receiver, and I loved watching Jerry Rice. I'd watch his highlight reel over and over and visualize myself doing the exact thing he was doing.

The night before games, I would see myself on the field. I'd review every play in my head and imagine how I would run the routes perfectly, catch the ball perfectly, and run into the end zone every time.

A few hours before the game, I'd physically walk the field and see myself in position doing what I visualized and experience the feeling of making the big plays and winning the game. This process got me ready for anything and everything that might come my way and put me into position to create with my body what I had already performed in my mind so many times.

I do this every week for my personal life and business as well. This book is a perfect example. For years before writing this book, I would visualize myself walking into bookstores and seeing my book front and center on the big front tables right inside the doors. I would see myself at book signings, speaking in front of thousands of people and spreading these key lessons of greatness to leave a bigger impact on the world. I did this for years before I ever sat down to write one word of this book.

I also practice visualization before I call people on the phone, whether it's personal or for business. I envision what I want to create from the exchange—perhaps a particular result for a business deal, a feeling or experience I want the other person to have at the end, or how I want a controversial situation to resolve. I visualize the whole process.

Each night, I visualize what I want to accomplish the following day. Before giving speeches onstage, doing online webinars, and so on, I visualize what impact I want to have. You could do this before going on a date with someone, preparing a meal you want to create, or anything else you want to do in your life. Visualization is a powerful process. It puts your mind in a place to set you up for success.

Your Visualization Process

Create a clear space with no distraction. I prefer it to be in nature, which for you might mean at your favorite park or on the beach. Or you can do this in bed before you go sleep and right when you wake up. I've also been known to do visualization in the shower with the water rushing down and imagine myself in a waterfall.

Allow yourself to relax and be calm. Breathe relaxing breaths. Now visualize whatever you want to see as complete. Nothing negative, only positive outcomes.

If your vision is to be a father, visualize yourself holding your newborn baby, what that looks and feels like.

If it's to have a relationship with your soul mate, visualize yourself embracing that person, both of you smiling, and being whole and complete in that moment.

If it's to have a successful business, see yourself making the deals, walking into your office, helping your customers.

In each process, really dive into what it feels like: What does it smell like and taste like? What color is it? What sounds are you hearing?

The key to visualization is to see whatever it is you are envisioning as complete. Then ask yourself how you feel in that moment. What do all of your senses feel?

You can play music in the background if that helps you relax, or the process can just be silent.

I recommend you do this for at least 5 minutes every day, visualizing the outcome you have set out (no vision is too small or too big for this process). I also recommend doing this before attacking any big opportunity in front of you. Take a moment to visualize what you want to create before you enter that moment.

EXERCISE #2:
Meditation—The 15-Second Centering Breath

If the point of visualization is filling the mind with an image of where we intend to end up, meditation is about clearing the mind of everything else—all the extraneous distractions, obsessions, doubts, and trifling matters that keep us from focusing. It is something we need to do every morning when we wake up and every night before we go to bed (at least I find my days more powerful and intentional when I do it morning and night). You live the day of a champion by beginning as one and ending as one.

The key to meditation is to focus on your breathing and be aware of your breath. You want to unplug and simply breathe. Breathe in joy; breathe out stress. In joy, out stress. Allow yourself to feel connected to the world, to the universe, and, most important, to yourself. Anything that gets you disconnected from business, career, stress, and the rat race is great for you.

My favorite breathing exercise is something I've taken from another of the greats I've had the privilege of learning from, sports psychologist Jim Afremow, PhD. In his book *The Champion's Mind: How Great Athletes Think, Train, and Thrive,* Jim talks a lot about the importance of breathing to perform like a champion.

"Under perceived pressure, we tend to hold our breath, and then we not only don't have the oxygen to our system that we need but also our muscle tension increases," Jim told me when we talked. "Muscle tension is the number one enemy in sports. If you're a swimmer, you're going to go slower. If you're a pole vaulter, you're not going to jump as high. Deep breathing helps to clear our mind of stress and expectations, and it relaxes our body. I think it's important to have either a meditation practice or, at the very least, to take a deep breath throughout the course of your day and notice whether you're breathing easily and deeply."

15-Second Centering Breath Process

1. Breathe in through the nose if you can for a count of one, two, three, four, and five, expanding the belly.
2. Then hold it for a count of one and two.
3. Then breathe out through the mouth for a count of one, two, three, four, five, six, seven, and eight, releasing the air in the belly.

Be prepared, this is a big breath. It's not something you're doing all day. This is just to reboot your breathing. But the key is the exhale. It's a little bit longer than the inhale, and that's where you get the relaxation response.

"When we think about taking a deep breath, most of us just think about the inhale—taking that big inhalation. That's actually the stressful part," Jim made me understand. "Getting all that air out, that's the relaxation part and really helps you to feel your best."

You will be surprised how you feel if you do this before bed or before an important meeting or event. When we focus on our breathing instead of the things that stress us out or that we are afraid of, we don't allow the stress or fears to creep in. Go ahead and try this exercise right now and repeat it for four cycles (1 minute in total). Let me know how you are feeling at the end of it by sending me an e-mail at lewis@schoolofgreatness.com. Anytime you are feeling overwhelmed or stressed, come back to this breathing process for 60 seconds. It will give you the clarity you need to take your next step, wherever you are.

If you want an another free guided meditation from

me to get you in the right frame of mind for your day, then check out schoolofgreatness.com/resources for additional resources.

EXERCISE #3:
Mindfulness

If you don't already have one, I want you to start a gratitude journal. I want you to write down your thoughts and express gratitude. Each night in your gratitude journal, be mindful of what's really working for you and what isn't working. Take the time to jot down everything you are proud of and excited about and to acknowledge yourself for these amazing things you've done. Then write down what you are committed to doing to move those things you are proud of forward.

For example:

Today I closed the biggest deal of my life. I'm proud of myself, and it's a dream come true.

Tomorrow I will continue to bring my [product/service/ message] to the world to help more people.

Next write down all the things that you reacted to or that weren't effective and failed to get you the results you wanted. Look at what was missing from you in those moments (patience, love, courage, confidence, etc.). What are you committed to creating and who are you going to be moving forward in those kinds of moments?

For example:

Today I didn't close the sale.

What was missing was that I didn't have the confidence in my product and I was too pushy about the result of the sale instead of showing my care for the potential customer.

I wasn't committed to being in a relationship with that customer. I will be connected the next time to understand their needs and wants instead of focusing on the result I want.

We think about these things in our heads constantly, but rarely do we ever speak them out loud or put them down on paper. Verbalizing and writing down these thoughts allow you to be aware and mindful of what you are creating on a daily basis and see what's working and what's not working in your life. Over time, you will create a record of what has worked and what has failed; what you have done to make things better and what you have (or haven't) done that has made things worse. You will spot patterns that will blow your mind. So even if you don't see results right away with this mindfulness exercise, recognize that you are doing the work to make results happen in the near future, when you will be ready to see and accept them.

EXERCISE #4:
Emotional Intelligence—Be Present and Know Thyself

The first key to greatness is having a vision for your future, but the best way to supercharge that vision is to be emotionally present so that you can give your full attention to the moment.

I love to salsa dance, and not just because it involves beautiful women who know how to move. I love it because it's something that forces me to be totally present and in the moment. If you are worried about how you look, whether you are doing something wrong, not being good enough, or if you're thinking about literally anything else other than that moment in that place, then your partner will be able to tell (and so will everyone watching you). To be good at salsa requires that you be present, that you be connected to what you are expressing in the moment and fully connected to your partner so you can lead them (or be led) to the next step or move during the song.

In that way, life is a lot like salsa dancing. You must be present, connected, and focused on making someone else smile if you want to create something meaningful each day. It's not always easy. Sometimes it can be scary to focus and put yourself out there like this, but it's extremely powerful and can create magical results!

You must learn to be confident with who you are and believe in yourself. All champions, even if they are scared, fall back on their belief in themselves and the work they've put in to get them where they want to be.

Emotional intelligence involves being able to shift in the moment and be aware of your emotions so they don't control you or hold you back; rather, you use them to move you forward. The more you develop emotional intelligence, the better able you will be to handle emotional situations in all areas of your life—with yourself, family, friends, and intimate relationships and in your career.

In short, emotional intelligence is the ability to understand and regulate your emotions and the emotions of others and be able to use that power to guide your thinking and behavior.

One of the key aspects of emotional intelligence is knowing yourself: your strengths and your weaknesses. Feedback is the vehicle you can use to achieve that. Feedback is information about how you are showing up to others and in the world. With that information, you develop greater, more highly tuned awareness of your strengths and weaknesses.

Step 1

List your five strengths and five weaknesses.

Some examples of strengths

Powerful	Loving
Passionate	Committed
Disciplined	

Some examples of weaknesses

Controlling	Fearful
Lack of discipline	Judgmental
Overanalytical	

Step 2

Contact three people who will be brutally honest with
you and give you feedback about what they believe are
your top five strengths and five weaknesses. When you
have this information completed, put those lists side by
side and identify what they have in common. This will let
you know what you need to reinforce in your life (your
strengths) and what you need to work on moving forward (your weaknesses). Also, it will let you know how
calibrated your opinion of yourself is. Do you view yourself more or less the same as others view you, or are you
completely delusional in either the positive or negative
direction?

If you can be brutally honest with yourself, and you
can find good people who will be brutally honest with you
as well, this exercise is sure to give you a lot to reflect on.

Bonus exercise: Call someone from your past with
whom you once had a strong bond but are now no longer
in contact (a former partner in an intimate relationship,
a friend from your past, or even a family member you
lost touch with). Ask them as well to share what they
consider your strengths and weaknesses with you. Their
responses may surprise you, and I dare you to do it to
see what lesson you gain from that conversation.

COACHING TIP

You have always been great, because you are unique, and *you* will never happen again in the history of the universe. Most people don't believe in themselves or their abilities because they don't understand how insanely special they are. In fact, we all are special, and only we have the ability to believe in ourselves. Others can be there for us and cheer us on from the sidelines, but even with all the support in the world, some of us still sabotage ourselves. In the game of life, we hold the controls. We are the players who make the plays. Our inner voice—our belief in ourselves—is what determines our mindset. And our way of thinking sets us up for failure or success.

You have a choice. You can think average and get average results or think like a champion and reap remarkable rewards. Which one do you want? It actually takes only a little more effort to believe in yourself than it does to put yourself down. Make the decision to spend that energy on improving your mindset and doing things that give you confidence rather than bring you down. Always come back to understanding how unique and powerful your gifts are in this world. You are the one who needs to understand this first before anyone else can. Now go make it happen!

GET GROUNDED

If I could attribute one thing to my success, it would be the topic of this next chapter: hustle. It started all the way back in seventh grade with the middle school basketball team. All I wanted was to make that team, to be part of something, and to contribute in a positive way. I wanted to be accepted and valued. I think we all want to feel worthy in the eyes of others, like we matter and that what we do is meaningful. This basketball team was my first opportunity to experience that in an organized fashion. Neither my body nor my skills had developed by that point, but more than anything, I didn't want to get cut (getting picked last was a big fear of mine, as it had happened before), so I ran around like a madman, dove everywhere on the court, and showed that I had all the passion and hustle in the world (a dream quality to any smart coach). I was willing to sacrifice my body unlike any other kid out there. While others didn't want to look stupid or were afraid to get hurt, I had a different vision. My efforts paid off. Not only did I make the team but I worked my way into a starting spot on my first-ever team sport.

It takes more than just hustle to be great, but you can't be great without that burning desire to do what others are unwilling to do. Sacrifice, in some form, will be a necessary part of the process, and whoever is more willing to sacrifice for the hustle will always succeed in the long run. Prepare yourself, as it's time to embrace the underdog within and step into your greatness.

CHAPTER 4

DEVELOP HUSTLE

No one is going to hand me success. I must go out and get it myself. That's why I'm here. To dominate. To conquer. Both the world and myself.

—**Unknown**

In 1991, a college sophomore studying music in the American Midwest made the mistake of selling some drugs to the wrong person. Until then, he hadn't done much more than smoke pot and sell some of it to his friends. Petty vandalism at his high school was as high stakes as his criminal career had been. Then, as these things tend to go when you're just 18 years old, he tried to push the envelope and test his boundaries. He started experimenting with hard drugs like LSD. But he was naive, and the brashness of youth got the best of him. He sold some of that LSD outside his circle—to an undercover policeman. And as if his luck couldn't get worse, like a scene out of a TV movie of the week, the judge, under pressure to make an example out of this young man, sentenced him to 6 to 25 years in prison.

It's a faceless, timeless story that transcends race, class, and region. A young kid makes a mistake that forever changes their lives and their family's lives as well. We are all too familiar with how stories like this usually end: The kid spends their most impressionable years behind bars and comes out worse than when they went in. Life on the outside is too difficult to contend with; habits learned on the inside are too difficult to shed. They reoffend; their crimes escalate. The cycle continues.

This story, however, is a little different. Because this young man didn't go back to jail. In fact, after being released in less than 5 years on good behavior, he went on to become one of the best jazz violinists in the world. He left prison with a fire lit underneath him—to practice, to repent, to humble himself, to hustle, and to do whatever it took to make something of his life. No task was too small, no gig was too tiny, no potential fan was too disinterested for him not to give it everything he had. And he did.

The story is a little different for another reason, too. That young man's name is Christian Howes. He is my older brother.

Chris's journey taught me one of the most important lessons I ever learned about greatness: *how to hustle.* No, not that kind of hustling—selling drugs on the streets. The good kind. The kind that makes you sweat and makes other people nod their heads and marvel at your work ethic. Of course, like most lessons in hustle, it did not start as all silver lining and no black cloud. It was born where necessity met adversity.

Chris went to jail when I was just 8 years old. It was a shock to all of us. I remember sitting in the car outside the courthouse, asking my mom what was happening and her just crying. I remember asking her why it was happening, but my parents wouldn't tell me, not until after he got sentenced. When the news spread and the neighborhood found out—which doesn't take long in a small suburban Ohio town—none of the mothers would let their kids play at my house. I was in second grade, and despite having my parents and my sister still there, I felt alone and helpless.

In retrospect, Chris's situation should not have been a surprise. Despite the musical genius that certified him a child prodigy, he'd been a troubled youth. "I hadn't been motivated," he said. "I didn't have goals. I was just coasting. It was jive." Still, none of what happened to him made any sense to me. It didn't feel real. I thought that only people who killed other people went to jail. Chris hadn't done anything like that. Plus, he didn't look like what I thought prisoners would look like when I was a little kid. He didn't have a smashed nose like a Bugs Bunny gangster. He didn't have a wild beard and crazy tattoos across his back like an outlaw biker. He was just Chris, my big brother, whom I looked up to. He was still a great guy, he just made some dumb decisions. And what's more, when I saw him in person, behind bars, he was still a hero to me.

That didn't alter the fact that this was a stunning and traumatic part of both of our lives. Prison isn't something a family usually comes back from intact. Chris would always be a convicted felon. I would always be the kid from the broken home with the older brother who went away. We'd always be "that family" down the street. If Chris had fallen into the trap that so many others do, he could have absorbed the trauma and spent his years in prison getting angrier and more resentful of the world around him. He could have blamed the cops, the system, or our parents. He could have just given up. The list of places outside of yourself to lay blame is virtually endless if you look hard enough. Instead, he made a clear choice: to overcome the stigma and the setback of his incarceration by resurrecting his life.

He rededicated himself to his musical gift. "When I got in there," he told me later, "I had a purpose. I knew I wanted to be a better person. I wanted to be a man and do something with my life." Music was going to be that something. He persevered against the monotony and put himself in the right mindset, scheduling time with the prison band every week. The only white guy in a group that played gospel, rap, R&B, and soul (Chris grew up playing classical music), he embraced the challenge and earned what would be considered a kind of prison master's degree in music appreciation and the resilience of the human soul. He developed an unrivaled set of skills—both mental and physical—that would set him apart in the world of jazz and spark his unlikely ascent.

To survive in prison, you have to overcome your own mind and protect yourself from everyone around you who is trying to take what's yours (your stuff, your dignity, your sanity, your freedom). You have to be strong, not just physically but also mentally—you can't give in to despair and lethargy. To have a chance on the outside once you're released, the challenge is the opposite—to break through the walls of people who don't want to give you anything you need (respect, opportunities, the benefit of the doubt). When Chris got out, he had to overcome the reality of being a convict and the opinions, biases, and fears of people he encountered as he tried to build his career. He did this with a freakish combination of passion and hustle—both in prison and out.

SHAMELESS URGENCY

There's a great quote from Publilius Syrus, a former slave in Roman times, who became famous for his wisdom. "Do not despise the bottom rungs in the ascent to greatness," he said. He was basically saying, you are not too cool for school. That was Chris. When he first got out, he would perform anywhere. He started by playing for free at local restaurants just to put himself out there and build a name for himself. Then he'd do hotel lounges, late-night dive bars, tiny jazz clubs with five people in the audience. He would play whatever time slot they'd give him for however long they needed him to play. He would put 100 percent of his blood, sweat, tears, and soul into each performance to blow the doors off the place. His passion ended up blowing the doors off places that didn't even have doors.

"When I got out, I was not afraid to promote myself," Chris said. "Most people can't get over that fear. In the arts world, you're supposed to stay cool, man. Just do your music, and it will come to you. I said, 'Fuck that. I know what I want to do. I want to be a great jazz violinist, to go onstage with great musicians,' and so I pursued it zealously."

After his final number in every set, Chris would get back up on the mike and promote the hell out of himself. He would thank them all for listening to his music, then grab his stack of CDs and go up to each person at each table in the club trying to sell copies. He was not afraid to put himself out there. Once when I asked why he sold his work so hard, never taking no for an answer (even when the person was saying, "Not a chance!"), he told me: "There's no shame in my game." And he was right. He was shameless but genuinely putting himself out there, and it worked—people bought his music.

Chris was tapping into something that I think 18-time Olympic gold medalist Michael Phelps described best when he talked about his swim training with Piers Morgan on CNN: "If you want to be the best, you have to do things that other people aren't willing to do." I watched with amazement as Chris pulled out all the stops, persuading customers to invest in his recordings and his future. It was about survival for him, about providing for his young family by

doing work that he was fortunate enough to be exception-
ally passionate about. He was willing to do whatever it
took: "You have to chase opportunity whether you are an
entrepreneur or an artist—especially for me, because I
had to make up for so much lost time."

The irony is, we're all making up for lost time. That
is the essence of hustle in the pursuit of greatness—
doing whatever it takes and chasing opportunity with
great urgency, like your life depends on it. Because it
does. Greatness is really the survival of your vision
across an extended timeline, based on your willingness
to do whatever it takes in the face of adversity and to
adopt the mindset to seize opportunity wherever it
lives. After all, greatness is not something that comes to
you; you go to it, and it's always moving. You slow down,
and it moves farther away. You stop, and it disappears
over the horizon.

Since those days in tiny jazz clubs and no-name festi-
vals, Chris has toured the world, been on the cover of
magazines, played Lincoln Center and Carnegie Hall,
and collaborated with greats like Les Paul, Greg Osby,
D. D. Jackson, and Spyro Gyra. His list of collaborators and
clients is literally as long as my arm. He was a professor
at the prestigious Berklee College of Music and set up a
highly successful jazz violin camp where professional violinists from all over the world come to learn from him. All
of that should have surprised me, but it never did,
because he understood the importance of hustle in the
pursuit of greatness.

GET UP AND DUST YOURSELF OFF

I was not a happy kid during Chris's years in prison. I was never the smartest kid in class. In fact, I was the opposite. I was ugly and awkward (at least until high school). I was lonely. I didn't have friends. I was picked last for everything. I remember telling my teacher a number of times, "I wish I was dead." I got called into the principal's office once in elementary school because I'd been getting into trouble. I said it to him, too, right there in his office: "I don't know what the point is. I probably shouldn't be alive." I didn't feel like I was ever going to matter.

I was 12 years old and smack in the middle of the worst period for most young guys—middle school—when Chris was finally released. It was the best day of my life. He called us on my dad's car phone in a 1988 Oldsmobile. "Order us a couple large pizzas, bro!" he said. "I am coming home!" When he walked in the house, he gave me this huge hug, and it was everything I needed. I had been so filled with all sorts of frustration and painful, confusing feelings. I finally had someone around whom I looked up to, whom I admired, who had also gone through pain and turmoil.

But it wasn't commiserating over our bad luck that was so important—it was his response to the negative circumstances and his ability to lift me out of the hole I'd sunk into. He didn't lie down and cry, like I so often wanted to (and did) as a little kid. He got up and hustled his ass off. He said to me at one point, "I can't go down any farther. I've already been to the bottom. I've embarrassed

myself and my family and let everyone down. There's
nothing I'm afraid of now, especially looking bad." In
those early days, when he was playing at restaurants for
free, it's not like he was calling ahead to schedule with a
booking agent. He would just show up. He would go door
to door until someone said yes. He created something
from nothing. He had to. His back was against the wall.
He was committed to his vision of being the best jazz violinist he could possibly be, and no amount of adversity
was going to stand between him and his ability to make a
full-time living at his passion.

Watching him do that—sitting there by his side as he
defined his dream, knocked down every obstacle in his
path, and then doggedly chased down greatness—was
utterly transformational for me, almost more so today, now
that I understand how special it was. Chris's passion for
music and the hustle he displayed reaching fans and making new ones are what inspired me to get off my sister's
couch in Columbus all those years later. For more than a
year, I slept on that couch, 6 months of that time in a full-
arm cast after a career-ending wrist injury that led to a
painful surgery during my first season playing professional
football. With no money to pay off my credit card debt
and student loans and no college degree, I was left wondering if I had any hope of regrouping and figuring out why
I was put on this earth, let alone of defining and achieving
the greatness within me. My whole existence had been
built on a foundation of becoming a highly successful
athlete, and even though I had achieved those early
All-American dreams, I was now languishing in self-pity

because I'd washed out of professional sports. My vision was dashed; I was depressed and lost.

What Chris's hustle after prison made me realize was that I wasn't depressed because my vision was dead. I was depressed because I hadn't done the work to pick myself up, dust myself off, and figure out what was next. The hustle wasn't over; it was just different and shifted in a new direction.

Soon after that epiphany, I reached out to a number of people for guidance—my father's friends, coaches, my brother (obviously, why not go right to the source?), even the headmaster of my university, a man named Stuart Jenkins. I admired his wisdom and his moral courage. Stuart was hired to make changes and improve the university, and his decisions to cut underperforming members of the faculty were not popular. But his efforts vastly improved the academic standards of the school, and he proved to be an effective leader. He would often say to me, "Is this serving you?" rather than telling me what was right or wrong.

During that period of uncertainty, Stuart suggested I check out LinkedIn.com, the social media Web site, which back then was just starting to get serious traction among business professionals. I saw all sorts of potential to connect with high-profile business owners and other professionals there, and I began connecting with people like a madman. I reached out specifically to people who worked in the sports business because I had just come from my own experiences playing professional football, and I figured that would be a strong connection point to people I'd barely heard of in some cases and, in each case, never met. Lucky for me, I was right and got a high rate of acceptance.

In the first year, I made 10,000 connections! It was crazy but incredibly exciting. I became what Malcolm Gladwell called in his best-selling book *The Tipping Point* a "connector." It didn't happen overnight—I built these relationships one by one with passion and energy. I would meet people in person, talk to them on the phone, introduce them to others seeking their skills.

It was around this time, with my professional sports career over and my cast off, that I started making a little bit of money by hosting "LinkedIn networking events" around the country. Over the following year, I hosted 20 events in major cities, where 300 to 500 people would attend. They were amazed at how this 24-year-old former pro athlete kid with no degree was able to get so many people to show up at these professional networking events. What they didn't know was that I was literally e-mailing my LinkedIn connections one by one to ask them to come to my events or join one of the groups I'd created to bring everyone together. I adopted the approach Chris took right after he got out of prison—there was nothing I wouldn't do. I'd already reached my bottom, so the only direction was up. E-mailing everyone individually wasn't sustainable at the rate I was growing, obviously, but it kick-started everything I'm doing now and taught me valuable lessons about hustle—first and foremost that you have to be willing to do the work that others are unwilling to do if you want to succeed when starting from a position of disadvantage.

I eventually built this presence on LinkedIn into an incredibly lucrative online business. I had no background in building a business, but I pulled myself up by the bootstraps, went with my gut, took advice from mentors, and worked my ass off. There were no days off, no coffee breaks. I applied Chris's hustle strategies to the launch of the business, adjusting his tested methods to the practical realities of building a different kind of business from the ground up. The end result: The money started flowing in, when only a couple years earlier, I had no clear idea how I would ever make any money.

My inner frustrations and early fears are what drove me to hustle. I didn't want to be a failure. I didn't want to remain unseen. I was going to work my butt off and go through as much pain as I needed to bear. This, in part, is what powers me through a bad meeting or a failure even today. Even more so today, I'm driven by my vision to inspire others to reach their greatness, and it's what keeps my hustle so strong even in my darkest, most difficult days.

THE CURSE OF DAVID: WORKING HARDER *AND* SMARTER

The best hustlers are all underdogs. Even if they're not, they view themselves that way. They have a chip on their shoulder, or they chase something bigger than they are, because it's harder to hustle—to give it your all—when you're in the lead. You have nothing to judge yourself against or chase down besides the finish line. You're

always more productive when you're the underdog—
when you're David, not Goliath.

Just ask Tom Brady. Brady is arguably the best quarterback in the NFL. He is a no-doubt Hall of Famer; he
has four Super Bowl rings, three Super Bowl MVPs, two
kids, and one beautiful supermodel wife. Yet he plays
with the fiery, junkyard-dog intensity of a Davidian
underdog every game because he's got a Goliath-size
chip on his shoulder. Not only did he come to the University of Michigan and land *seventh* on the depth chart (the
lowest-ranked quarterback on the team), but once he
battled his way into the starting job as a junior, he had to
fight off another quarterback, Drew Henson, whom the
coach platooned him with the entire first half of his senior
season. Then, in the 2000 NFL Draft, despite setting
records at Michigan and earning Big Ten all-conference
honors, he wasn't drafted until the 199th overall selec-
tion in the sixth round—a compensatory pick, no less—
by the New England Patriots. Actually, to say that the
chip on Tom Brady's shoulder is Goliath-size is an understatement. It is the size of the 198 guys picked before
him and the 29 teams who had four or five chances to
draft him but chose not to. He works harder than everyone to show all those people what's what. He is a true
David in that sense.

My middle name is David, so I've always naturally
gravitated to that biblical story and the position of the
underdog. In fact, I've felt like an underdog at nearly
every point in my life—ever since childhood, when I was
picked last for sports teams or, worse, not at all and

forced to play by myself alone after school because no one wanted to be my friend. It is part of what has driven me to outtrain anyone and be better than everyone, because I'm not always going to be the biggest, strongest, or smartest. And when that happens, I still have to figure out a way to win no matter the circumstances, whether that means having the most energy, passion, or desire. If I have to, I'll be like a banshee out there. I'm always willing to put in the time and energy because I remember what it was like in elementary school to be picked last for everything and feel like life wasn't worth living.

Hustle isn't about working smarter instead of harder. It's about doing both. Hustlers are better *and* badder. They take their place in this world, they don't wait or hope or pray for it to come or for someone to hand it to them. And it's that Davidian underdog chip on their shoulder that often gives them the extra push when greatness seems at its most fragile.

In this way, Chris is literally and figuratively my brother-in-arms. But my sister-in-arms is Marie Forleo. Marie is an author, a TV host, and a business coach. She calls herself a "multipassionate entrepreneur," which is another way of saying she's a junkyard dog who attacks everything she does with passion and hustles her butt off, even the stuff she doesn't love to do or she knows isn't going to be what she does for the rest of her life. And she does it for a reason.

"So many opportunities have come from me training myself to show up like a champ wherever I was," she told me. "I got my first job on the floor of a Wall Street trading firm because I did such a good job on this one person's cappuccino at the place I bartended during college. He was like, 'You care so much about what you're doing, what do you want to do after you graduate?' I told him I was a finance major but I couldn't see myself in corporate finance or behind a desk. He said, 'My brother works on the floor; give me your résumé.'"

Part of me couldn't believe that was all it took to get a job on Wall Street, but the other part of me knew from watching my brother, Chris, that you can never underestimate the power of hustle. It can unlock a ridiculous amount of opportunity and potential. Even after Marie left her Wall Street job, she continued to approach her life with the same energy.

"I taught hip-hop at Crunch [a fitness center], and I didn't think I was going to teach hip-hop forever, but I wanted to be the best hip-hop instructor I possibly could be. And because I taught a good class that was always filled, the higher-ups chose me to audition for a new Nike program."

The result? Marie became one of the first four Nike "elite trainers"—a group who got to travel all over the world. She didn't wait around hoping someone would recognize her talent. She shoved it right in their faces and made it impossible for them not to see.

"The opportunities that can come when you do that, you can't even predict," she told me. "When you show up with that attitude of 'I'm going to master this, I'm going to bring my A game,' you feel better. You have more energy, and the results are going to be better."

Once Chris got out of prison, he wasn't waiting for anyone, either. He didn't expect anyone to feel sorry for him or give him the opportunities he always dreamed of—nor could he in his industry—so he went out and hustled to make his vision a reality. Les Paul, the famous guitarist, once remarked, "It used to be you could hardly find a good jazz violinist, but nowadays there are four or five really good players." I think that competition from all these players who hadn't lost 4 years on the inside was what drove my brother to be the best. It's what made him hustle—to try to carve out a space for himself. And if Les Paul is any judge, Chris's work has paid off, because even though there are now four or five really good players, he also said, "There is nobody better than Christian Howes." If there was such a thing as a mike drop in jazz violin, this would be it.

FALL IN LOVE WITH THE ART AND PAIN OF THE HUSTLE!

A Japanese proverb says, "Vision without action is a dream. Action without vision is a nightmare." You need both vision and action to achieve great things. Vision guides you; action propels you. But most people settle for the dream, because it is free and easy. It doesn't require action or hustle, which comes at a heavy price sometimes. Most aren't willing to pay that price. This is yet another place where true greats distinguish themselves. Muhammad Ali once said, "I hated every minute of training, but I said, 'Don't quit. Suffer now, and live the rest of your life as a champion.'" Training? Suffering? That is the hustle.

Earlier I joked that if you don't have a vision that gets

you out of bed in the morning, go back to sleep until you find one that does. I mean that—it's absolutely critical. At the same time, truer words have never been spoken than by Jonathan Swift when he said, "I never knew a man come to greatness or eminence who lay abed late in the morning." Your vision is what makes you want to get out of bed. Ultimately though, you have to do it. And you have to do it over and over and over again with every ounce of energy that you have, even on those days when you hate the suffering the most—especially on those days, in fact.

Do you think during the high school football preseason I enjoyed doing three-a-days in the heat of the summer while other kids were off at the pool flirting with girls? Hell no! It sucked like no other. But I'm a two-sport All-American, I became a pro athlete, and, as a result, I play for my country with USA Team Handball, the men's national handball team. Those guys who were taking it easy at the pool when I was killing myself . . . what are they doing now and what do they have to show for that? I have no idea, and neither does anyone else. And that's the point.

If there is someone who has a right to hate the hustle more than anyone, it's Kyle Maynard. Born with profound physical limitations, every day that he perseveres against the adversity laid before him should be a victory. But not for Kyle. His vision for greatness required not only that he stand up to those who stood in his way but that he put in the work to prove them all wrong and succeed in spite of them. The authorities who didn't want him to fight mixed martial arts and the parents who objected to him as a high school wrestler were no match for someone who was zero percent talk and 100 percent walk. He pushed through day after day and was so earnest in his efforts that he got his shot in both arenas. ESPN didn't just magically hear about Kyle's climb up Mount Kilimanjaro—he didn't wait for good things to come to him. He went out and hustled, promoting it to whoever would listen. He brought attention to his cause with unrivaled passion because he believed in it and wanted his message to get out.

Shawn Johnson talked to me about hustle and passion, too, particularly with respect to talent. So many people think they can skate by on talent to reach their goals and accomplish their dreams. She is firmly in the camp of Team Hustle. Why? "You can be the biggest or the most talented person in the world, but if you don't love what you do, then it's not going to show and it's not going to work. And you don't necessarily have to have the greatest talent, but if you work for it and you love it, then you'll have better results." She is absolutely right.

If Shawn is on Team Hustle, then its captain has to be Angel Martinez. He is pure hustle. He was a great runner not because he was naturally talented but because he was willing to work harder than everyone else. He had grit. It began when he was a grade school kid in the Bronx picking up hundreds of two-cent glass bottles to buy a new seven-dollar pair of Cons. It continued to work for him on the cross-country team in high school as much as it did years later when he was going from meeting to meeting trying to turn Reebok into a global footwear brand.

The difference, I have discovered thanks to so many of these great mentors, between those who achieve greatness and those who cannot get beyond mediocrity is very closely tied to how hard they hustled. My brother showed me the power of hustling to change even the most challenging of circumstances. Chris wasted his natural talent for years, getting distracted by drugs, trying to impress too many losers at school. He went to prison and nearly lost everything. But his passion for music and becoming a better man to make something of his life gave him the direction and the energy that propelled from a prison cell to the practice room every day for 20 years.

I know that's easier said than done. So far, I've only given you the Nike approach to hustle—Just Do It. But hustle is somewhat of a difficult discipline for people to wrap their heads around (most hard things are). It's not something you can learn. It's something you just have to put into action.

The question is, what holds people—what holds you—back from developing it? It's usually not a lack of energy. Everyone is capable of hustling. But we always seem to leave something in the tank; we go at half speed. We don't have that sense of shameless urgency. We won't get up and dust ourselves off. We won't embrace the harder, smarter work of David to the Goliath of our competitors or our haters. We won't just grin and bear it and do the work. Why? In a word: *fear.*

Fear of looking bad: We don't want people to see us sweat or struggle, and we are afraid of what people think about us.

Fear of failure: We must remind ourselves that we will fail 100 percent of the time we don't try.

Fear of success: At times we fear our success greater than our failures, because some of us don't want to be put in the spotlight or be required to lead when we succeed.

So how do we step away from these fears in our heads and step into action? Part of the process is understanding, as the 18th-century English writer Samuel Johnson did, that "true greatness consists in being great in little things." Baby steps, essentially. Turning small things into great advantages through hard work by flexing the hustle muscle. It's a skill all the professors in the School of Greatness have mastered at some point along their paths. They understand that you don't just go from starting quarterback of your high school team at 16 years old straight to the Super Bowl, because even if it were allowed, they know you aren't ready for it at that age. You must go through the necessary progression to gain experience, wisdom, and years in college before you are allowed to compete at the NFL level. Then only a small percentage of the best players in college football make it to the NFL. Then only one team a year can win the Super Bowl. It takes years and years of doing the right things to set yourself up for the chance to achieve greatness for something at that level.

All that being said, it's never too late to start. It's never too late to hustle in pursuit of your vision. In 2011, the Jazz Journalists Association nominated my brother, former inmate #260873, for Violinist of the Year. In 2012, he was selected for the prestigious Residency Partner Program from Chamber Music America for his educational outreach work with school music programs. In 2014, the US Embassy in Kiev invited him to tour Ukraine and serve as a cultural ambassador. It wasn't raw talent that got him there; it was his relentless drive to make up for the lost time he'd frittered away as a young man. And that is the lesson that has made all the difference in my life. If I could give one piece of advice to a budding entrepreneur, it would be that—just one word: *hustle.*

EXERCISE #1:
What-If Scenarios

When my students notice their minds falling to any of these fears that hold them back, I give them an exercise to calm their thoughts and get them back to a grounded place of principles and vision that will lead them into action.

With pen and paper or a journal, find a comfortable and quiet place where you won't be interrupted.

Think about your vision and your goals. Imagine the hustle required to make them a reality. Now write down all of the things you are afraid of if you throw yourself headlong into the hustle. Allow yourself to experience the feeling of fear while you write these things down.

What if I look stupid?	What if I go broke?
What if I mess up?	What if I ruin the
What if I lose my	relationship?
investment?	What if I get fired?

With each what-if, write out all the things that could go wrong, including the worst-case scenario. *What if I get fired . . .*

> . . . and my wife leaves me?
> . . . and we lose the house?
> . . . and we have to live in the car?
> . . . and my friends stop talking to me?
> . . . and I can't find another job?

Let it all out onto the paper. Experience the fear with each possible outcome. Now redirect each what-if into a potential positive outcome. *What if I get fired . . .*

> . . . and it turns into a better job in a few months?
> . . . and I can use the severance to take a well-needed family vacation?
> . . . and I can spend a month reconnecting with my kids?

Turn every what-if into a positive redirect of "what could" be created instead. Again, your vision won't come to life without your assuming some risk or taking some action. Mistakes will happen no matter what. It's part of the game; it's part of life! Fear is a necessary component of that—it helps you calculate the risk—but you can't let the fear make the decisions for you. You must feel the fear, process it, and do what you need to do to achieve what you've set out for yourself.

A lot of times we don't hustle because we are afraid of the negative potential outcomes. But if we use that fear, process it, and shift our thinking toward the positive potential outcomes, we can turn that fear into faith. When people hustle, it's not because they have no fear—

it's because they've harnessed it instead of letting it harness them.

EXERCISE #2:
Working the Hustle Muscle

There is a popular saying in entrepreneurial circles that goes something like this: "Entrepreneurship is living a few years of your life like most people won't, so that you can spend the rest of your life like most people can't." What they're talking about is hustle. Hustle is about taking consistent action over a period of time in order to build momentum and create the kind of leverage that makes things easier in your life over time. Not surprisingly, this is also the recipe for greatness. It's achieved through consistent action over a long period that begins well before the season begins or opportunities arise.

Everything I've ever been successful at has involved, whether I knew it at the time or not, massive action by being clear about my vision and doing whatever it takes to achieve it. But hustle isn't just about taking consistent, massive action every day toward what you want—it's about taking smart action as well.

There are four smart areas everyone can and should be hustling in:

1. Your body
2. Your mindset
3. Your relationships
4. Your skills

Hustle is a muscle. It's something that takes time to develop into a powerful momentum-building machine. To develop your hustle, you must embrace it and fall in love with the process. The daily journey of developing yourself is, in fact, hustle itself, and over time you'll see massive results from it. Here's how I approach it, plus an exercise on how to develop your hustle muscle.

1. Your Body

Do one thing every day that makes your body healthier and stronger. Something that is painful (the good kind of pain) and requires you to push yourself physically at the gym, on the bike, or during your run. Something that makes you feel uncomfortable, that you'd rather not do. It's this consistent habit of doing something that is painful and uncomfortable that will increase your pain threshold and make you stronger in all areas of your life (in Chapter 5, we cover the steps to mastering your body even more).

2. Your Mindset

Do something every day to improve your mindset and your way of thinking. The greatest minds question everything. They see the world where anything and everything is possible (even if it sounds absolutely crazy). This process could be:

- Reading a thought-provoking book
- Listening to an inspiring podcast
- Going to a workshop
- Learning from a coach or mentor

- Asking questions about everything (allowing yourself to be curious)
- Understanding that you can learn something from everyone
- Studying meditation and different philosophical ideals

3. Your Relationships

A leader is someone who understands that relationships are the key to success in business and life. How well you understand people, your compassion, and your ability to flow through others' emotions in stressful situations influence how deep you can go in relationships. But it's also important to know and be known by the influencers in your industry to achieve greatness in your career, business, or brand. If you follow any of the following steps, you'll be setting yourself up to win in the area of relationships.

- Connect with three new people each week in your industry in person, by phone, or online.
- Connect with three influencers each week (any industry).
- Share a meal with three people each week (breakfast, lunch, or dinner), like the great Keith Ferrazzi recommends in his book *Never Eat Alone*.
- Go to one group event every month—a networking event, breakfast meeting, mastermind group, etc. (Mastermind groups have been a key ingredient to my making seven figures in my business, and I dive into how to join and start your own mastermind in Chapter 7.)

- Send video messages online or via phone to your connections. Don't do this just on birthdays but also make it a point to follow up to see how you can support them with anything they are doing, and ask what their biggest challenges are right now. For example, I like to e-mail friends and just let them know how much I appreciate all of the work they are doing in the world, and I talk about something specific I see them doing at that time. Don't ask for anything in return or do it for any reason other than to show how much you care. This will stand out in their minds and deepen the relationship.

- Ask questions and make the conversations about others, not about what you want. When you focus on giving support to those you trust and believe in, they will almost always want to offer support in return.

- Show up at industry conferences, trade shows, and summits.

For many of you, this will come naturally, but for others who are more introverted, this will require stepping out of your comfort zone and developing a stronger mindset (as in Chapter 3). If you are going to events in person and feel uncomfortable at first, simply find a friend whom you can attend with to ease the anxiety, or start with smaller group events and grow from there (more on relationship building in Chapter 7).

4. Your Skills

Whenever you are in transition or you feel stuck, it's not the time to hunker down, it's the time to hustle and learn new skills. The more skills you have, the more you have to offer in any situation—it's like you've added a new tool on your tool belt to handle any situation in business and life. I'm constantly learning to master new skills and taking on new challenges each year. These are just some of the skills I've picked up over the past decade based on the dreams and passions I have in my life.

- Learning the guitar
- Salsa dancing
- Joining Toastmasters and improving my public speaking
- Picking up a new sport (Team Handball)
- Learning how to write books
- Learning how to build Web sites and grow a following through social media
- Learning to be a coach and workshop facilitator
- Podcasting and editing
- Learning meditation
- Learning acrobatic yoga
- Learning CrossFit, yoga, and different styles of strength and fitness training
- Learning how to make money
- Learning how to invest money and start and launch a business
- Learning how to manage my emotions and let go of my reactive ego
- Learning breathing techniques
- Learning how to hire a powerful team for my business

All of these are things I didn't know how to do when I was growing up or in college. It took time to learn and master these skills, but now because I can pull them off my tool belt at any time and access them in different areas of my life, I'm able to get where I want to be much easier and faster.

Write a list of 10 skills you want to learn. Start with the one that excites you the most and create a game plan for how you will learn it over the next 6 months. It could be a new language, graphic design, a new instrument or hobby. Also think about the skills that will support you in your relationships, your mindset, and your body, as those will be key to supporting you on your path to greatness.

COACHING TIP

Will Smith once said in a sit-down interview with the great Tavis Smiley, "The guy who is willing to hustle the most is going to be the guy that just gets that loose ball."

Most people get stuck in life because they are obsessed with what could go wrong. I had the opposite experience growing up. Everything was already going wrong. I was made fun of a lot, I was picked last for stuff, I didn't feel accepted. Worrying wasn't an option. I had to take action to improve myself and overcome my fears if I didn't want to feel that insecurity anymore.

When you experience fear, move toward it. When you feel doubt, take the necessary actions to build your confidence. When you are afraid of being wrong or looking bad in front of others, be humble and vulnerable to create real human connection. The hustle takes action. It requires getting over yourself and how you look. It can be a beautiful journey if you give yourself permission to hustle like a maniac because what else are you here to do other than make the most of what you can be?

GET GROUNDED

Your body is everything. You may think being a little over-weight isn't that big of a deal, but on the road to greatness, it affects your overall energy and can be that one thing that holds you back with everything. Each body is different, but we all respond positively to a certain set of guidelines and philosophies. Throughout this chapter, you'll hear about these lessons from some incredible teachers who've studied the body (and the mind) far more than I have in all of my years as an elite athlete. I've been in great shape, and I've been in horrible shape, so I can speak to how much better my entire life is working when I'm on the path of body mastery. Your body is your home; it's time to learn how to keep it clean and free of clutter to fulfill the vision within you!

CHAPTER 5

MASTER YOUR BODY

If the body be feeble, the mind will not be strong.
—Thomas Jefferson

Rich Roll was a former NCAA Division I swimmer on some of those amazing Stanford University teams in the 1980s that produced a number of Olympians. After he graduated, he went to Cornell Law School and became a successful entertainment lawyer. He had a beautiful wife, a happy marriage, and a luxurious home near the ocean in Malibu Canyon, California, yet like so many fortunate, accomplished people who appear to have it all, he was not happy. It felt like there was a giant hole in his life from which his spirit and drive and passion steadily leaked out.

Despair is the word a lot of us would use to describe that state, and it can happen whether we have success or not. It's depression. Burnout. Exhaustion. Sick and tired of being sick and tired!

Rich was almost 40 years old and felt stalled out when he should've been at the top of his game. He knew he wasn't living up to his full potential. It's a phase that can hit at nearly any age. Midlife crisis. Quarter-life crisis. Whatever caused it, whenever it happens, it is the opposite of greatness.

"I was just unhappy," he said. "I felt ripped off, cheated. I'd done everything right and should have been celebrating, but instead I was unhappy."

Rich was working 80-hour weeks and bingeing on junk food. It was the only thing he had time for, and at the same time, he was so overworked, the idea of the self-control required to diet seemed laughable. He never had the time to work out and consequently gained 50 pounds. He broke 200 pounds for the first time in his life and kept going. Rich was in denial and rationalizing his deteriorating physical and emotional health.

One day he was climbing a flight of stairs at work, and halfway up, he had to stop. He was out of breath, felt tightness in his chest, and couldn't make it to the top. As a former athlete, this really hit Rich in the stomach—his increasingly flabby stomach.

We've all been there, where having given up on something or run into adversity we can't bear to face, we just pretend. We pretend we don't have a problem and just plain ignore it for so long that it takes an event like this at a moment like this to pierce through our delusions. We sit there paralyzed by grief and confusion: *How did it ever get like this? What happened between then and now that could possibly explain why I can no longer walk up a flight of stairs or play with my kids or sit comfortably in an airplane seat?*

At different times in my life, I've oscillated between

exercising like a madman and wanting to just say screw it and be lazy. Being healthy can be a lot of work, and it can be so tempting to procrastinate and kick the can down the road. But if you want to do great things, that is absolutely the wrong attitude. The path to greatness means being responsible to yourself and others.

In that moment, we have a choice. Unfortunately, too many of us choose to do nothing. To continue to pretend.

But Rich did not.

TACKLING THE IMPOSSIBLE

"I'm 39," he said to himself right there, "and I had to take a break walking up a simple flight of stairs. Something is really not right. I need to make some changes."

He decided in that moment this would be a new beginning in his life. It was this choice that put Rich *back* on the path to greatness.

What he did *not* do was decide to make a small change. A small change or an incremental commitment is too easily forgotten or abandoned. "I'll cut out soda." "I'll eat a salad for lunch." "I'll start Monday." Instead, he started fresh immediately—with a full cleanse to clear his body of the toxins and waste he'd been shoveling into it. He'd been treating his body like a toilet instead of a temple, and now he had to flush it out—and then repair the plumbing. He did this by cutting out all of the junk food and meat and eating a completely plant-based diet.

"The first couple days, I was buckled over, sweating, like I was in rehab," he told me. "It felt like detoxing off heroin or something; it was terrible. By the last couple days of it—and I don't know if you've had this experience—I felt incredible. Better than I'd felt in 20 years or maybe ever. That told me just how resilient the human body is. In a matter of a week, after treating my body so horribly with a terrible diet for so long, I felt better than ever."

The famous English billionaire businessman and adventurer Richard Branson has been asked for his best piece of business advice. His answer is always one word: *exercise.* Why? Because if you don't take care of yourself, you can't take care of your business. A stroll through the Forbes list of the world's billionaires is, with only a couple exceptions, a testament to this idea. Nowhere is the connection between physical health and business wealth more pronounced than with the current generation of entrepreneurs, represented most completely by author, angel investor, and human guinea pig Tim Ferriss.

Tim is best known for the number one *New York Times* best-selling book *The 4-Hour Workweek,* but he is just as passionate about human performance as people like Steven Kotler. His second book, in fact, was called *The 4-Hour Body* and introduced the world to a number of amazing ideas and practices. It shouldn't shock you that physical activity is very important to him, on many levels. "I find sports very helpful as a bookend to close out the day," Tim told me, "to do training at 6:00 p.m., where you are absolutely protecting that time as much as you would protect any other type of conference call or anything else. Not only does it set your body up physically for dinner and the rest of the night, but it also forces you to prioritize your day in order to get all your work done before you head to the gym." The energizing effect of both those things—getting your work done and getting the blood flowing—is a huge asset on the path to greatness.

I think Rich was feeling the truth of all that advice, because he was finally starting to fire on all cylinders again. He loved the way he felt so much that he decided he would stay clean. For him, this meant that he would become a vegan. A significant number of monumentally successful businessmen and leaders have done this over the past 5 or 6 years to get healthier and more productive: Steve Wynn, Bill Clinton, Mort Zuckerman, Al Sharpton, Russell Simmons, Biz Stone, and John Mackey, the CEO of Whole Foods Market. Even Mike Tyson went vegan, and he was an ear-chomping killing machine!

With all the junk out of his diet, Rich made a commitment to exercise again. Not a little bit but a lot. His wife bought him a bike. He started swimming again. He hired a coach, because he was so serious about getting healthy that he wanted to surround himself with experts and good energy. It started off gradual, but at the end, Rich was putting in 25-hour training weeks. It became like a second job, as he had cut back on his law practice significantly to pursue his new lifestyle practice. In a relatively short time, he was an athletic machine nearing the best shape of his life.

And that's when it hit him: He was going to do an ultramarathon—which is essentially any distance-running event beyond a traditional 26.2-mile marathon.

"Two years prior, I couldn't make it up a staircase, and here I was. I had never done an Ironman; it wasn't like I was a seasoned triathlete. I'm a complete newbie. I was very inexperienced at this. I had a level of confidence that I could complete it, but I also had a responsible level of humility about what I was about to do. I wasn't there to win or anything like that. I was there to celebrate the fact that I was sober, that I had lost this weight and changed my life. That was really it."

Despite that humility—or perhaps because of it—Rich didn't just finish the race, he placed 11th. In his very first ultramarathon. You don't need to be an extreme sport enthusiast or an endurance athlete to appreciate the audacity and ridiculousness of Rich's accomplishment. It would be like taking up rock climbing as a New Year's resolution, training on a rock wall for a few months, and then going to Yosemite on the first day of spring and sprinting up the face of El Capitan like a spider monkey.

I found this transformation to be so inspirational and profound. Rich had mastered his body and taken back control of his life along the way. What I love the most about this is that Rich found his calling in life, and a new vision was born in the process. He's built an ultrasuccessful lifestyle business out of his passion. Now a best-selling author, he educates and inspires millions around the world through his books, widely popular podcast, vegan health products, speeches, and more. He turned adversity into advantage and ran with it, literally!

Rich said, "My whole life, I had chased the carrot. Go to the best school. I got in all the Ivy League schools; I studied hard." But where did it get him? Overworked, unhappy, and, worst of all, out of shape. "I was at the point in life where I was supposed to be celebrating everything that I had built," he said. But he couldn't. In his position, who could? Greatness isn't about working a lot or making a lot of money. It's about having purpose and being the best that you can possibly be. And how can you jump for joy when you struggle to walk up a damn flight of stairs?!

YOUR BRAIN ON JUNK

All the teachers in this book mastered their bodies in one way or another. I also spent some time learning from Daniel Amen, MD, a leading American psychiatrist, a brain disorder specialist, director of the Amen Clinics, and *New York Times* best-selling author, which added another layer to my understanding of why mastering the body is so important. It's not just about muscles. Your brain matters, too. Your mind and your body are connected; they are both part of your body. Are you taking care of them? As they say, garbage in, garbage out.

"Your brain is literally involved in everything you do. How you think, how you feel, how you act, how you get along with other people, and when it works right, you work right," he told me. "When it's troubled, though, for whatever reason—toxic exposure, head trauma, drug abuse, lack of oxygen—that's when you start getting sadder, sicker, poorer, less successful."

The problem so many of us have is that we completely ignore the role of our brains in the health of our bodies. "If you never look at the brain," Dr. Amen warned, "you may never know what is going on with you." And when that happens, you can find yourself in a nasty cycle of poor physical health leading to poor emotional health, which in turn leads to worse physical health, and so on and so on.

When I was bummed in my own life and career, I went through a similar bout of lethargy and felt that slow slide toward unhealthiness. What was really tough about it was that it happened so gradually. I steadily gained a pound a month for close to 2 years. To make it more confusing, I also started to become successful (financially and in my business) around that time. That made it harder to see through my own carb-driven haze and question my habits. After a 2-year period of hustling, barely making much each month, I remember making $6,200 on my first webinar and feeling like I was the richest man in the world. I started eating like a rich man, too. After that moment, the money started to roll in, and so did my fat rolls. I was eating 7,000+ calories a day (to be fair, I was working out, too, but it was all out of balance). Worst of all, I had sugar after every meal, which is a huge no-no even if you're interested in only a basic level of health. I just wasn't taking care of my brain or my body. When I look back on it, I know that I wasn't the best I could be. I wasn't thinking or feeling as clearly as I could have.

It turns out, according to Dr. Amen, that when your weight goes up, the size and function of your brain go down. It wasn't until my move to New York to pursue Team Handball and my dream of representing the United States in the Olympics that I finally snapped out of this slump, and it was only because the waistband on my underwear finally snapped back at me. I knew I was getting pretty heavy. My face was so wide my family and friends started to joke about it—they called me "Flewis" . . . *Fat* Lewis—but when I couldn't wear my underwear anymore without the waistband snapping back and rolling down under my belly like a slap bracelet, that was enough. I stepped on a scale for the first time in a long time, and the digital display shouted "254" back at me in big, red, angry numbers. I decided in that moment to cut out everything bad for the next 30 days (Rich Roll–style).

I didn't have any sugar, gluten, or dairy for 30 days. I'm not saying this is for everyone, nor was it recommended to me by any health expert or doctor; it's simply something I wanted to do to create a new habit for myself, because I understood the power of creating positive habits when something isn't working the way you want it to (more on this in Chapter 6). I lost 28 pounds in the first 28 days and felt better than ever, so I decided to do it for another 30 days and dropped a couple more pounds. I didn't change anything else, and I was still working out the same way . . . it was all from cutting my intake of the stuff that wasn't working for me. I dissolved Flewis by drinking (and falling in love with) green juice every day, eating foods that were organically grown and taken directly from the ground, and eating organic, grass-fed meat. Between choosing the right foods and remaining dedicated to my workouts, I've never since worried about gaining the pounds back.

I now have sugar and sweets from time to time, but my diet is much more balanced, and my weight (and health) is where I want it to be. My life is better every day because of it. And the work I put into mastering my body has made all the other decisions I have to make and the work I have to do that much easier.

But naturally—and my brother, Chris, was an example of this—people put a lot worse stuff in their bodies than sugar: drugs, excessive alcohol, and nasty chemicals. We deprive ourselves of sleep or even have "natural" addictions like gambling and sex. This has a real and tangible effect on your ability to perform. Forget about the kind of flow state that Steven Kotler describes in his books—that's way outside the realm of possibility with these negative influences at play, because they can quickly and easily destroy your body and tap-dance on your brain. So stop abusing yourself!

SLEEP YOUR WAY TO THE TOP

Just like Rich Roll, 5 years ago Ameer Rosic, Canadian kettlebell champion and an expert on sleep optimization, was in a bad place. He suffered from deep depression, he dabbled in alcohol and drugs, and his outlook on life was horrendous. "I had no meaning in life at all," he told me. "I felt like there was a dark hole, an abyss, in my heart. Then life hit me on the head with a hammer."

The epiphany came when he woke up and realized that much of his struggle was due to a lack of sleep. He was up into the late hours nearly every night partying, getting very little sleep, thinking he was a superman who could take on anything. His physical and emotional health began to suffer, and with that his life suffered tremendously, too. He knew he had to do something, so he began to learn about circadian rhythms and the importance of getting the proper amount of sleep. "Everybody needs to realize, we are like batteries," he said. "Sleep recharges you. It increases and balances hormones, strengthens your immune system, gives you clarity, gives you focus, and so much more." The more he researched, the more Ameer realized that sleep was the pivotal factor in achieving optimal health, ahead of diet, ahead of exercise, ahead of everything.

And for Ameer, the turnaround could not have been more stark. "I have somehow encapsulated so much passion in my soul, in my being, and it is because of the way I sleep, the way I eat, and the way I treat my body, because when you treat yourself first, everything else follows and everything else is greater," he said.

The impact of proper sleep wasn't just physical either. Ameer raised his IQ, became the Canadian biathalon champion in kettlebells (the national sport of Russia— don't ask, I was as confused as you are), and built a business helping others optimize their health. Ameer put it best when he said, "If you want to run a business and you want to do good in this world, if you want to deliver value in this world, it's all about treating one's self first. When you treat yourself first and you create that perfect vessel, you then have the ability to affect so many more people globally."

It's crazy how important a foundational habit sleep is! As Shawn Stevenson, sleep specialist, author of *Sleep Smarter: 21 Proven Tips to Sleep Your Way to a Better Body, Better Health, and Bigger Success*, and another great mentor whom I have had the privilege to learn from, put it: "Sleep is something our genes expect of us." He calls it vitamin S, which perfectly explains the additive and restorative role of sleep in our lives. When he talked to me about the information in his book, he could not overstate just how detrimental a lack of sleep can be to every aspect of life.

"We have a thousand things going on in our lives, and sleep is often one of the first things we tend to omit," he warned. "We don't understand that by lacking that high-quality sleep, we're actually *demolishing* our ability to achieve at a high level in everything else in our lives." (emphasis mine)

This is especially true for entrepreneurs, many of whom wear their marathon coding sessions or back-to-back all-nighters as badges of honor in the race to start-up success. To you folks, Ameer has some shocking news that you need to take to heart: "Around 2013, a study came out that showed people who stay up 48 hours or more, which many people do in these crazy stressed-out days we're living, have the same blood sugar as a diabetic." As a diabetic! "Now can you imagine," he continued, "what happens when this gets compounded? Day in, day out, year after year after year. It's going to end up in something not very beneficial."

I think we can nominate that last sentence from Ameer for the Understatement of the Century. It was definitely a "holy crap" moment for me, I can tell you that.

If you're like a lot of people who are struggling with turning your dreams into reality, with realizing your vision for greatness, right now you are probably saying, "Look, I have a demanding job. I have kids. I can't exercise 25 hours a week like Rich Roll or go to bed at 10:00 every night and sleep 8 to 9 hours like Ameer Rosic. I don't have the time, I have commitments." Well, Rich did, too. "We need to be extremely selfish a few hours a day and take care of ourselves and our bodies," he said. Echoing Ameer's point, he continued, "You can't help someone else if you are not taking care of yourself."

I've learned that it's a lot like when you're on an airplane and they say, "Put your own mask on first, before assisting others." You can't help anyone if your brain is oxygen starved or, worse, you're already dead. The same principle applies to taking care of ourselves so that we might help others. We need to make sure we're really taking care of our bodies, physically, mentally, and emotionally. We need to make sure we're getting all of our needs met, that we're going after all of our wants and desires. Those don't come last, they come first—no matter how selfish that might feel. When they come first, everything else follows quickly after.

Rich said, "I'm a better person when I'm taking care of myself in this way. There's a certain part of me that feels like that's what I'm supposed to be doing. I'm wired for it. I'm happier, I'm more productive, I'm a better husband, and I'm a better father when I am training and taking care of myself in that way."

WHAT IS POSSIBLE WHEN YOU MASTER YOUR BODY

Chalene Johnson, a *New York Times* best-selling author and a world-renowned fitness coach, has trained hundreds of thousands of people and sold millions of copies of her workout videos. She witnesses firsthand what's possible when you take ownership of your health. Her students send thank you messages on a regular basis sharing what they've created in their family lives, careers, and personal relationships due to her training. Some people find it difficult to change their lifestyles with years and years of bad habits; trust me, I get it. But Chalene, now a close friend, said to me, "Anything and everything is possible with a plan. If this [healthy body] is what I'm interested in right now, what am I willing to give up?" If you want to make a change, then something needs to actually be different in order to get better results. Meaning, what vices in your life would you need to remove to improve your health and your body and gain all that is possible with a mindful lifestyle?

For Rich, his relationship with his family improved when he made physical health a priority. He was content. He was happy. Much as Ameer's work with sleep became more than just a curiosity, Rich's success at training and running quickly became more than a hobby. He built an entire lifestyle business out of it, for crying out loud, and he became *great* in more ways than one to boot.

I know this sounds crazy, but I am convinced that a major reason many people don't achieve greatness or even reach for it is because they just don't have the energy. They aren't taking care of themselves. We all need to do a better job of this, for ourselves and in support of others. Remember, it doesn't matter how great your vision is, you cannot muster the will to overcome adversity or marshal the energy to hustle tirelessly if you're out of breath or stuck on the couch.

Your greatness problem might just be a health problem.

And just because you haven't taken care of yourself in the past doesn't mean you can't and shouldn't start right this second. Rich was 40 when he got serious. We can't turn back time and start over, but we can choose how it will end, and it is never too late to take the first step in the right direction. That's what mastering your body is about. The past is irrelevant—what matters is where you go now. Maybe your road will end on (or include) many miles of high-endurance running. Or maybe it's just getting in better shape so you can play with your kids. Or maybe it's eating right so your head is clear and fresh so that you can think without the fog.

Regardless, mastering your body is a fundamental, foundational part of your journey toward greatness. It is the engine that powers the runaway train of your vision, pushes you over obstacles, clears a path for you to focus, and fuels the hustle that takes your dreams even further than you imagined possible when you first dreamed them. Do not take advantage of your body. Do not take your brain for granted. As Ameer described it to me, "We are like banks, and there's a mechanism in our brain called sleep debt that actually accumulates the seconds, the minutes, the days that we miss out on sleep. And just like with a loan that doesn't get properly serviced, one day the bank will come knocking on your door, saying, 'Hey, Lewis, well, you owe us about 2 to 3 years of catch-up time.'" And just like with real banks, that knock almost always comes at the worst possible time. In the pursuit of greatness, mastering your body is all about not letting your body write checks that your brain can't cash.

The idea of entering a CrossFit gym or training like an elite athlete may be as terrifying to you as giving a speech was to me when I went to Toastmasters the first time. But that doesn't let you off the hook from mastering your body in the School of Greatness. If you want to play a big game in life, you need the energy it requires physically and emotionally to take on every challenge and obstacle that stand between you and your vision. Here are three things you can do to master your own body starting right now!

EXERCISE #1:
Take a Picture of Your Body . . . Naked!

If you really want to inventory how you view yourself— what you like and don't like—there is one place to start. See yourself naked, literally, and then take a picture.

Accepting (and loving) your body is the first step. Take a picture of yourself naked and evaluate the parts you love and the parts you want to improve on, and write them down. Notice where you're putting your negative energy and focus on accepting those aspects of your body. Only then will you have the positive energy you need to make the improvements you want.

Without your accepting responsibility for your body the way it is at this moment, the unhappiness or negative energy becomes a source of your results. Anything that's based on fear ends up in fear. By accepting and loving my body, I've got the positive energy I need to stay on a workout plan and lifestyle diet that others might struggle with. When you love your body—or maybe more accurately, the person *inside* your body—it's much easier to stay committed to a vision than to do something out of fear and self-loathing. From this place, you are able to choose to lose weight because it matters to you, not because how you look matters to others.

EXERCISE #2:
Develop a Fitness Lifestyle Plan That You Love

My goal for this book is to open you up to any and all possibilities. No matter where you are on your fitness journey, each step can be one in the right direction. Know that your body should not hold you back but only move you forward in achieving your vision.

First, carve out the time—write it down in your schedule. This should be a minimum of 5 days a week for at least 30 minutes per day. This will create a routine and reinforce a commitment to physical health as part of your lifestyle. It doesn't matter what time you exercise during the day; at this point, the most important thing is to do it at the same time every day to make it a consistent habit. Pick a time that works well for you and your lifestyle. I prefer mornings because it kick-starts my day and puts me in a positive mental space, since I've completed something before I've really even begun my day. As my mom says, completion is powerful.

Second, start moving and get active. I always incorporate things that I love into my fitness program, because that is the easiest way to get and stay motivated. As an athlete, I play a lot of pickup basketball, go running, do sprints, lift weights, swim in the ocean, and try different boot camp–style workouts because that's what gets me excited when I exercise.

This doesn't mean you need to spend 2 hours crushing your body every single day. The important thing is not to get paralyzed by the overwhelming expanse of the fitness industry. Whether it's jogging in the neighborhood, walking with purpose to the café to get your daily tea, or stretching for a few minutes in the morning, every little bit of movement counts. Remember, this is a journey, not a destination.

Third, find an accountability partner for support. This could be a friend, spouse, trainer, or even pet (yes, make a commitment to keep your dog in shape as well!). You are that much more likely to commit when you have someone else holding you to your word. Many people hate working out, which is why they don't stay with it. If this is where you are, then an accountability partner might be the perfect thing to help you stay committed and make working out more fun.

Last, I've learned to do one painful exercise every day so that I can expand my comfort zone and take my body and mind to new levels. So do something each day that makes you uncomfortable. This doesn't mean you should go and try to pull a muscle because it's painful. You essentially want to do something new and/or difficult that is consistent with what you are striving for with your body. Although I love certain things about my workouts, I never keep to the same routine for too long. Change is good. I always push myself to a level of discomfort that eventually becomes painless and rewarding.

This probably sounds like I'm telling you to search out crazy, exotic exercises that target muscles you didn't know you had. Nothing could be further from the truth. Your goal when it comes to painful exercise is really doing anything that makes you sweat and sends your heart rate up—doing pushups (or any lift or exercise) to failure, repeating hill sprints with minimal rest, or simply working out harder than the previous day. It's simple: *Push yourself!*

I'm personally a big fan of interval training. This includes making your own workout of four to six exercises that you'll do for 45 seconds at a time with a 15-second rest between each exercise for as many rounds as you want.

Example of an Interval Workout

45 seconds: pushups   15 seconds: rest
15 seconds: rest   45 seconds: lunges
45 seconds: air squats   15 seconds: rest
15 seconds: rest   45 seconds: situps
45 seconds: jumping rope   15 seconds: rest

Do this for four rounds (or adjust the rounds and time for each exercise to push yourself however you want). You can get as creative as you wish with this simple workout plan and add in any type of exercise, with weights or just your body weight. You can do this at home, at the gym, or wherever is most convenient for you. Make sure to change things up and keep it fresh. Depending on how many rounds you do, the workout will take roughly 30 minutes with light stretching before and after.

The key here is to do something that you enjoy (even though it will be painful) and find someone to make it fun with you. For more workout resources and options, go to schoolofgreatness.com/resources.

EXERCISE #3:
Find Out What's MISSING

Aubrey Marcus, my good friend, a health expert, and CEO of the nutrition company Onnit, designed this exercise exclusively for you! With his focus on total human optimization, his method for mastering your body begins with finding out what's missing from your health and lifestyle. It's so important that he has turned it into an acronym to guide your progress (MISSING). Figuring out where you are physically and physiologically in each of these seven areas is critical to your health and your ability to effectively pursue your vision on the path to greatness. Use this exercise as a guide to see what's currently missing from your health and adjust each area as needed.

M—Mineralization

The body is made up of a variety of minerals. Every single system in our bodies requires adequate minerals to function properly. We get these in the foods we eat. Ask yourself where your foods are coming from. Are your fruits and vegetables organic and locally grown? Is your beef grass fed? If the answer is yes, you're on the right track. Trace your food back to the source.

One of the best ways to return minerals to your daily diet is to use Himalayan salt. Regular table salt contains only three minerals: sodium, chloride, and iodine. Himalayan salt has anywhere from 65 to 85 trace minerals. The expression "worth one's salt" comes from Roman times, when soldiers were given an allotment of salt as their *salarium,* which is where we derive our word *salary.* To function efficiently, it was essential that soldiers replenish the salt lost by their bodies during long marches. Having the right salt could mean the difference between life and death.

I—Inflammation

A lot of top doctors now are saying that pretty much all disease stems from some type of inflammation. The reason is that the body has to combat inflammation, just like you would combat any other type of pathogen. When the body is using resources to deal with inflammation, it has far fewer resources to deal with immune response and proper function, and thus disease can grab a foothold. Managing inflammation is incredibly vital.

Paying attention to those inflammatory processes is important. Inflammation can even come from poor digestion! One thing that can be valuable in dealing with inflammation is using proteolytic enzymes. Proteolytic enzymes go through the body and start to break down any kind of dead proteins that are lying around the body and stimulating inflammatory responses. Utilizing a good proteolytic enzyme can be a major benefit to mastering your own health. (My personal recommendations for enzymes are at schoolofgreatness.com/resources.)

S—Stress

As discussed in Chapter 2, stress is a part of the human experience that we need to manage. We don't realize the physical cost of being under chronic stress. Stress releases a hormone called cortisol, which reduces immune function. Stress is fine if temporarily you need to run away from an animal, hit a deadline at work, or do something that requires a short burst of all of your focused energy. If the stress is chronic, however, the body is severely limited in how effectively it can deal with any number of stressors. Stress will eventually burn out your adrenal glands, and through a variety of chemical processes and substitutions, you'll start to produce fewer of other hormones that are essential for optimal living. So managing stress is incredibly important.

Now take time to write down what you do to manage stress. One of the simplest ways to reduce stress goes back to our meditation exercise in Chapter 3. It's been shown scientifically through a number of studies that deep diaphragm breathing will naturally release your stress. So focusing on your breathing is an important way to release stress.

Here are a few examples of what I personally do and don't do to manage stress.

DO	DON'T DO
Meditation	Smoke
Physical activities	Drink
Listen to music	Binge on TV
Change my environment	Overeat
Dance	Oversleep or lounge for days

S—Sleep

Sleep is probably the most important health tonic you can provide your body. It is the time to repair, restore, recover, and rejuvenate. Sleep is the key. There are great books, like *Sleep Smarter* by Shawn Stevenson, that talk about the different ways to improve your sleep. First and foremost is understanding that the body is designed to sleep during the night and be awake during the day. If you can optimize your schedule to get 7 to 8 hours of sleep during the night so you are fully awake during the day, you've taken the first big step.

Once you've gotten yourself on a better schedule, the next step is to optimize sleep itself. Photosensitive elements of the eye trigger melatonin production—that's the hormone responsible for letting you know that it's time to sleep and for helping the body fall asleep. Additional light in the late-evening hours short-circuits the melatonin process. So minimize artificial light sources like late-night TV and smartphones. No electronics in bed! Track your sleep nightly. Early to bed, early to rise, and get 7 to 8 hours of sleep nightly. It's that simple.

I—Inhalation

Our meditation exercise should reinforce the importance of breathing. Inhalation is one process that we do constantly throughout the day, and if we stop, we're dead. We don't realize how crucial getting oxygen to our body is. We just take it for granted. But not all breaths are equal.

If you're taking shallow chest breaths, you're not adequately oxygenating your body for optimal health and stress management. So paying attention to your breathing, using that as a rudder to navigate different health modalities, is key. Breath can help you deepen your meditation, it can power you in your workouts and in your training, and it can keep your body more alkalized, which will improve your mineralization. Breath is incredibly important and too often overlooked in the health picture.

If you get the chance when you have an extra minute (maybe while sitting in traffic), simply focus on your breath—those full diaphragm breaths that go deep down into your belly. The benefits to your health can be massive. Are you breathing optimally? Could you use more cardiovascular fitness? It starts here.

N—Nutrient Density

Nutrition in America has been calorie focused for a long time. What we have learned over the past couple decades, though, is that calories are not as important to health and having a great body as nutrient density. You can get 500 calories from sugar or you can get 500 calories from a grass-fed rib eye; your choice will have a vastly different effect on your body. How many nutrients are you providing your body? How many green vegetables? How many healthy fats, like coconut oil and avocado and olive oil, with their omega-3s and omega-9s? What kind of nutrient density does your food have? What doesn't have nutrient density? Make sure your meals are balanced and rich in nutrients. Water is the most essential nutrient; without it, human life cannot survive. Make sure you are staying hydrated. Are you drinking enough each day?

G—Gut Health

The gut is the cauldron of health. This is where your digestive system works to convert minerals and nutrients into fuel that will sustain a healthy body. From the very first doctor, Hippocrates, to doctors in the present day, medical practitioners have always been aware of gut health, but it's something that is only now getting its proper respect. Matter cannot be created or destroyed, so how do we grow or change? We grow by assimilating nutrients from our food and building our bodies and regenerating our cells by using those nutrients. Poor digestion can lead to inflammation and what's called leaky gut syndrome, where food particles escape through the gut barrier and trigger an inflammatory response.

Gut health is influenced by the probiotic flora in your gut, also known as the gut biome. These microorganisms are important for digestion. Additionally, many of the neurotransmitters and hormones that are responsible for your mood, your happiness, and everything that makes you feel great are either affected by or originate from the gut. Most of our serotonin production comes from the gut. Our immune cells are produced in the gut. Having a healthy gut biome—one that works symbiotically with the body—is vital for your immune function, for your mood, and for your health.

So when you're looking to master your body, pay attention to what you're MISSING. When you aren't missing anything, only then can you say you've mastered your body. Your goal at that point is to maintain where you are for as long as you can!

For the complete guide to figuring out what's MISSING from your health, along with resources on supplements and products to optimize your body plus my personal fitness plan, go to schoolofgreatness.com/resources.

COACHING TIP

Listen, I'm not perfect. My weight goes up and down sometimes. I don't always eat perfectly. Like most people, I love sugar and sweets. But I'm sick and tired of seeing people who have given up on themselves! The only difference between those people and me (and you, I hope!) is that I'm willing to put in the work and experience the pain necessary to keep my body and mind in shape so that I can perform throughout the day on a high level, live the life of my dreams, and pursue my vision come what may.

If you aren't getting what you want in life and you are out of shape, don't think for a second that those two things are unrelated. It's time to say, "Enough is enough." It's time to admit, "I'm sick and tired of feeling sick and tired." It's time to get up and do something every single day that makes you sweat and gets your heart racing. Put yourself through some type of daily discomfort, whether it's for 5 minutes or 50 minutes. Do something that is so uncomfortable that it starts you on the process of getting your body where it needs to be, and then maintain that by falling in love with the feeling of that pain. Yes, your vision and relationships and dreams depend on it, but most important, so does your life. It's time to step up and make your body great!

GET GROUNDED

Our habits shape who we become and the results we create in the world. In my life, I've cultivated habits that supported me and others that brought me down. We've all been there. Unfortunately, most of us don't know how important our habits actually are. The most successful, fulfilled, and vision-focused individuals in the world have daily rituals and habits to which they attribute a significant amount of their success.

If you want to achieve greatness in your life or your business, then everything you do needs to be done with a purpose and for a reason. It doesn't take long to form a new habit, but it can slip away from you just as quickly. True greatness comes from the intentional act of doing something positive over and over and over again. It's time to take a look at the habits you've been forming and begin forging a new path right now by applying some of the habits of the most successful people in the world.

CHAPTER 6

PRACTICE POSITIVE HABITS

Successful people are simply those with successful habits.

—Brian Tracy

rmchair quarterbacks love to yell at athletes who "waste their potential" or "take their gift for granted" or "don't hustle" or "don't act like a good role model." This is usually just empty projection, aimed at great men and women who have accomplished more than the fans can ever dream. But sometimes there is truth to it.

Anyone who has ever tried to make it in sports can tell you that while they were out at practice leaving everything they had on the field, there were other athletes using merely a fraction of their capabilities. Guys like NBA All-Star Allen Iverson (who, during an infamous press conference where he was being judged for missing practice, said, "I'm supposed to be the franchise player, and we're sitting here talking about *practice*?!") and National Football League All-Pro Charles Woodson were notorious for giving the bare minimum to get by until the lights came on. Woodson's ability as an All-American, Heisman-winning, All-Pro NFL cornerback was so freakish, so otherworldly, that he didn't dial up his practice habits until 10 years into his now 18-year professional career, and even then he only did it because he realized he was setting a bad example and creating bad habits in some of the younger players who looked up to him. He didn't do it because he didn't need it to compete at an elite level—a fact that drove his coaches on every team he ever played for stark raving mad.

This is not a story unique to the playing field. Poor practice habits—or preparation problems, as I like to call them—transcend the world of sports and affect us in our jobs and our relationships. Doing the bare minimum at work. Rushing to complete a task at the 11th hour because experience has taught you that you don't need the previous 10 to get it done. Forgetting your partner's birthday and running around the day of for a present that doesn't feel like you forgot. Crash dieting to lose 10 pounds before going on a beach vacation. We do these things because we've gotten away with them in the past. We were fast enough, smart enough, young enough, lucky enough. We lean on experience and ability, not on proper preparation. We have poor habits, and sooner or later our luck is going to run out.

One of my most inspiring teachers let his poor habits get the best of him. He is actually a guy with a story very similar (minus the fame and millions of dollars, of course) to Charles Woodson's. His name is Graham Holmberg, and I played college football with him. Practice after practice, week after week, season after season, I watched him get by purely on his physical prowess and agility, a substantial gift he was bent on wasting. I was glad he was on our team (you don't want to be on the other side of the ball from a guy like Graham), but I was also jealous and angry at the same time. Despite what seemed like unlimited athletic potential, reaching for true greatness didn't seem to be on his agenda. Instead, Graham preferred to party, chew tobacco (on the sidelines during practice even!), stay out late and sleep in late, chase women, and enjoy himself. He had no ambitions beyond being pretty dang good and having fun.

You might be saying to yourself right now, "Wait, that sounds pretty awesome!" And it is, or it can be, at least for a while. Who doesn't like to have fun and tear it up every once in a while? But that's the operative phrase: *every once in a while.* If that's all you do, eventually it gets boring, especially when it doesn't produce anything lasting or when talent can no longer bridge the gap that bad habits create.

Now others of you might be asking a different question: "Well, what if you don't have any talent? What then?" First of all, that's garbage. Every single one of us has talent churning away inside; you either have misdiagnosed yours, denied it, or taken it for granted. But second, talent—at least of the kind I'm talking about with Graham—isn't destiny. Sure, talent can make greatness easier to achieve, but greatness is not the exclusive domain of the talented. Greatness is the result of visionaries who persevere, focus, believe, and *prepare.* It is a habit, not a birthright.

Unfortunately, because he was so supremely talented and so much had been given to him at birth, Graham ignored the power of habits that his parents, teachers, and coaches tried futilely for years to drill into him. Or maybe a better way of saying that is, he let his life be ruled by those bad habits. And as I have come to learn after talking with true greats like Angel, Shawn, Ameer, and my brother, the number one way to waste your talents is to allow bad habits to take over. The consequences of a life led by bad habits are inevitable.

TREADING WATER

Now you wouldn't think that Graham would be the teacher we need. He never approached the kind of greatness we all saw in him, and over time he became deeply unhappy. But Graham's story doesn't end there—it gets worse and then better. When he left school, he didn't go pro. He didn't go semipro. He didn't go anywhere! He stayed right where he was, like all those people who peaked in high school, never left, and watched life unspool in front of them. It was almost like Graham was the real-life Al Bundy from the famous 1990s sitcom *Married with Children,* whose greatest achievement in life was scoring four touchdowns in the 1966 city championships for Polk High. And it was all downhill from there. Like Al, Graham was basically treading water. Treading water is not a growth strategy. It doesn't get you anywhere. There is no progress with treading water. All you're doing is fighting to stay in one place, with enough of your head above water to keep from drowning.

That was exactly where Graham was one day a few years later, when he learned that a close cousin had been killed in a car crash. Something in Graham clicked. It was like he finally woke up from the stupor he'd put himself in, and instead of treading water, he began to kick and paddle with purpose. I've never seen someone turn his life around as quickly as he did, giving up all his vices cold turkey and going to the gym nonstop. On this new path, he developed the workout and lifestyle habits that would eventually turn him into the world champion at the Cross-Fit Games and earn him the label "the world's fittest man."

But the greatness he achieved in fitness is not what we can learn most from, or at least what I learned most from. Graham's turnaround was rooted in his mind. He became intensely spiritual and devoted to his faith. He became a baseball coach at the high school his beloved cousin had gone to. He opened his own CrossFit gym, where he offered Bible study on the weekends. He married and started a family. He turned the adversity that stopped him cold in his tracks into a new vision where positive habits fueled an amazing transformation that affected all areas of his life.

"It was like, I don't want to be a hypocrite to these kids, and inspire them and coach them up and teach them the right habits, if I'm doing bad stuff as well. I made a decision to just wipe that stuff out of my life and not let it control me anymore," Graham told me.

For Graham, that meant cutting out everything from chewing tobacco and drinking to other less tangible but equally toxic sins: jealousy, anger, ingratitude, ego. That is the tricky secret about habits—they are best built or changed one by one, but eventually, you have to get to all of them if you want to be great. In the quest for greatness, there is no substitute for developing positive habits.

AN OLD GREEK'S ADVICE

Aristotle said, "We are what we repeatedly do. Excellence, then, is not an act but a habit." That old Greek understood how important positive habits are to overcoming adversity and enduring the quest to become a champion. I have learned that champions aren't just born; champions can be made when they embrace and commit to life-changing positive habits.

Having known Graham for more than a decade and watching how he made a conscious shift to that new path, I decided to examine my own habits. I saw how quickly positive habits built strength and resulted in a deeper sense of belief—in myself, in my vision, and even spiritually.

This process wasn't easy at first. I never got into any of the obvious things we think of when we talk about bad habits—drugs, drinking, or smoking—because from an early age I saw what they did to my brother and realized I didn't want to make those same mistakes. I wasn't perfect by any stretch (and achieving greatness isn't about being perfect anyway), but my bad habits were less clear to see or less straightforward to understand. Thanks to a lot of introspection and coaching from greats like Chris Lee and Tony Robbins, I finally came to see all the bad habits I'd developed starting as far back as my time on the middle school basketball team.

- Beating myself up
- Being ungrateful
- Failing to acknowledge positive growth
- Being overly judgmental (toward myself and others)
- Disrespecting my parents and family
- Staying in unfulfilling relationships too long
- Eating poorly
- Not exercising regularly
- Keeping a messy living space
- Swearing like a sailor
- Staying up all night
- Sleeping in all morning
- Cheating on homework and tests
- Reacting to situations in a way that upsets others
- Getting by without practicing

It took a lot of time and constant feedback to realize what wasn't working in my life, and it will be an ongoing journey until the day I die. Over the years, I began adding positive habits and noticed a dramatic change in my results and the way I felt internally as well. Some of these include:

- Constantly expressing gratitude
- Smiling at as many people as possible

- Going to bed early
- Getting 7 to 8 hours of committed sleep
- Making my bed in the morning
- Staying organized
- Acknowledging myself and others
- Loving people wherever they are on their personal journey
- Eating clean
- Training my body
- Saving and investing my money wisely
- Meditating
- Visualizing my results and creating a game plan
- Respecting others
- Investing in my personal growth
- Preparing before big moments
- Surrounding myself with inspiring people

Staying consistent with positive habits can be a challenge. I still go back and forth on them. There have been many times where I was working out intensely and in the best shape of my life, and then for whatever reason, I got off track. Before I knew it, 3 or 4 months would go by, and all of a sudden, I'd find myself in the same position as Rich Roll—exhausted halfway up a flight of stairs!

The key to surviving and then thriving after these moments is to not beat yourself up when you do break a habit. Rather, you need to reconnect to your vision to refamiliarize yourself with why it's important to stay true to your positive habits in the first place.

A habit and its results can change fast, so it's crucial

to set yourself up to win and do what works for you to stay on track. For some, that's journaling the habits you kept and the habits you broke and creating rewards and consequences for yourself when you do. For others, that's hiring a coach to keep you accountable or finding an accountability buddy or friend with whom you can work on these things together. For still others, it's finding a mastermind group where you are all constantly challenging yourselves to stay on track.

The tricky part about habits is that any one of them (good or bad), when you look at them individually, doesn't seem all that critical. It's when you take them in combination or as a whole that they become incredibly powerful. They can easily and shockingly thwart the same amount of progress that they can create. This is why we admire people with great self-discipline. It's not because they were born great. It's because they learned the power of habits and applied that power to create a lifestyle that supports the best version of themselves.

Almost everyone knows the famous (and mythical) story about Michael Jordan getting cut from his high school basketball team. Not only did he use that as motivation (in reality, he got demoted to JV as a sophomore), but he cultivated an entire regimen of positive training habits that built him into the greatest basketball player to ever play the game—including spending every off-season adding a new move to his repertoire to make himself more unstoppable.

James Altucher, the great entrepreneur and writer, has talked openly for years about hitting rock bottom over and over again. His brilliant book, *Choose Yourself!*, is all about the positive habits he's developed to pick himself up off the floor and be more successful than he was before—from writing down 10 ideas every day to his now famous "daily practice" in which he works on and calibrates his physical, emotional, mental, and spiritual health. My former teammate Graham Holmberg did the exact same thing to turn his life around.

Now, I don't want you to think this is all about morals. Though morals are important, this is really about human optimization—not avoiding sin. Ironically, it was Eric Thomas, the inspirational speaker and "hip-hop preacher," who made this clear to me when he pointed out a simple bad habit that almost everyone has: getting distracted. Think about how hard it is for us to stay on task these days; from social media to e-mail, there is an endless pull on our time.

So Eric set out to change that tendency in his own work. He told me that he practices a "no interruptions" policy when he is being creative: "When I get started, I don't care if it's my wife, my children, they know that from a certain time frame, I'm going all in. And I can't go all in answering the phone. I can't go all in watching TV. I can't go all in with those kinds of distractions swirling around me." This has helped him craft messages that have reached millions of people around the globe.

Meanwhile, he pushes back at entrepreneurs and artists who can't seem to create work that resonates.

"It's because you're not in abstraction," he said to me. "You don't have that moment of your day—I don't care if it's 10 minutes or 4 hours—where you shut the entire world out. No Twitter, no Facebook, no Instagram, nothing. For that time, you're going all in. Once you come out, then we can do Instagram. And I'll be honest. Your content probably would be stronger if you had that time of isolation, of solitude, where you give yourself a chance to think. You give yourself a chance to go in, and when you go in, you go 120 percent. That's my ritual."

Really, it's a habit. An excellent habit. The beauty (and curse) of habits is that once they are formed, they are hard to break. Consciously pursuing great habits consistently will click you into autopilot on the path to greatness.

MAKE YOUR BED, CHANGE YOUR LIFE

I'll give you another example just to make it clear how simple and small good habits can be: Make your bed. In 2014, Admiral William McRaven gave an amazing commencement address at the University of Texas at Austin. In the speech, he focused on the critical nature of making and inspecting a sailor's bed each morning. This might seem like some petty, officious quirk of military regulations at first. After all, isn't that what your mother bothered you about every morning? But when you hear it from Admiral McRaven, it becomes the definition of a positive habit. It's a way to start off your day with an accomplishment and encourage you to keep tackling the tasks of your day. And furthermore, as Admiral McRaven said, "Making your bed will also reinforce the fact that little things in life matter. If you can't do the little things right, you will never do the big things right."

Admiral McRaven was not the first person to stumble onto the power of making your bed every day. Gretchen Rubin, the habit expert and number one *New York Times* best-selling author of *The Happiness Project,* has talked on her blog about making your bed since way back in 2007! In fact, of her millions of readers who worked on their own "happiness projects," she reported that making the bed had the biggest impact on their happiness. Her explanation for why this was the case, which she wrote about a few months before the release of *The Happiness Project,* echoes Admiral McRaven's words in many ways.

> First, making your bed is a step that's quick and easy, yet makes a big difference. Everything looks neater. It's easier to find your shoes. Your bedroom is a more peaceful environment. For most people, outer order contributes to inner calm.
>
> Second, sticking to any resolution—no matter what it is— brings satisfaction. You've decided to make some change, and you've stuck to it. Because making my bed is one of the first things I do in the morning, I start the day feeling efficient, productive, and disciplined.

I have to be honest, when my first company had its first million dollars in sales, one of the few splurges I made was to hire an assistant. I'm embarrassed to say that one of the things I had that assistant do every morning was make my bed (hey, at least someone was developing the habit!). But as I learned about the importance of positive habits, I stopped this. I realized that by having my assistant do a task like this for me, I was depriving myself of an opportunity to practice a positive habit that could kick-start my day on my own personal path to greatness. And now, every morning when I wake up, I make my bed—starting my day with some satisfaction and discipline.

HABITS OF HIGHLY SUCCESSFUL PEOPLE

Here is the thing about positive habits: It isn't that important which habits you practice, as long as they are beneficial and they work for you. What matters is that you commit to them and that you do them every day. Just like developing hustle is really about doing the work, practicing positive habits is about committing to a routine. A routine guaranteed to move you closer to greatness, especially if you develop positive habits related to the other lessons in the book: creating a vision, overcoming adversity, cultivating a champion's mindset, developing hustle, mastering your body, building a team, and being of service.

If you are like I was before I watched my friend Graham turn his life around and propel himself into the highest echelons of CrossFit like a blond-haired kangaroo, you might need help figuring out which positive habits are worth practicing. And to be honest, I still struggle with that at times. That's why, whenever I meet great people, I have a little habit (or I suppose it is a *meta*habit) I make sure I do. I try to observe them for positive habits to learn what made them great. I often explicitly ask about their habits when they appear on my podcast. The reason? I want to see which habits I should deploy in my own life.

In early 2014, *Entrepreneur* magazine ran a story about this very subject on their Web site. It featured a cool info graphic that showed the daily habits of the wealthiest people in the world. While making money is only one element of greatness (it is not everything by any means), there is something to be said for how their habits translate over to success in other areas of life.

These are their habits.

1. Maintain a to-do list.
2. Wake up 3+ hours before work (to set themselves up for the day).
3. Listen to audiobooks during commutes (or you can read, if you take public transportation, or listen to my podcast!).
4. Network 5+ hours each month.
5. Read 30+ minutes each day.
6. Exercise 4 days a week (I recommend 5 days myself, with daily movement, of course).
7. Eat minimal junk food.

8. Watch 1 hour or less of TV a day.

9. Teach good daily success habits to their children.

10. Make their children volunteer 10+ hours per month (I encourage you to do it with them to set the example).

11. Encourage their children to read 2+ books per month (I didn't read much as a kid and wish I would have).

12. Write down their goals.

13. Focus on accomplishing a specific goal.

14. Believe in lifelong educational self-improvement.

15. Believe good habits create opportunities.

16. Believe bad habits have a negative impact.

Following all of these habits won't guarantee that you'll become rich or that you will immediately achieve whatever form of greatness you are after, but they can't hurt, and they could very well be the springboard you were looking for!

I have incorporated a number of these habits into my life. Here are the daily habits I focus on the most.

1. Wake up early and say thank you for being alive another day (not 3 hours early, but it's an ongoing practice!).

2. Make my bed!

3. Meditate for 10 minutes.

4. Drink a green juice at breakfast.

5. Stretch and move my body.

6. Have a high-intensity training workout.

7. Eat organic, home-cooked meals.

8. Watch very little TV (for 4 years I didn't even own a set so that I would stay focused).

9. Focus on my goals and take action steps toward them.

10. Network with a purpose to give to others.

11. Acknowledge others and smile in every conversation.

12. Express gratitude throughout the day and the last thing before bed.

13. Work with a coach and mentors.

14. Constantly learn new information and skills.

Here are a handful of other habits I've picked up and adopted from some of the greats I've met along my path.

Be your word. I learned this when I was 11 years old from my father when he caught me stealing money one day. I remember lying to him about it and then feeling a tremendous amount of guilt and shame from the consequences of my actions after he found out the truth. He taught me that those emotions that made me feel sick inside were the result of not being your word. This meant simply doing what you say you are going to do when you say you're going to do it. Not lying is part of being your word. A friend of mine once said that as long as we are breathing, we will always be breaking our word. I'm not perfect, but it's something I strive for every day. The easiest way to make a person feel unappreciated or like they don't matter is to break your word to them or fail to follow through without a renegotiation (of what time you'll show up to a meeting, what they can expect from you, etc.). Being dependable to other people makes it easier for you to depend on yourself. Honoring your commitments to other people makes it easier to honor the commitment you have made to yourself when you created your vision for greatness.

Focus on gratitude. This is a habit I picked up from Tony Robbins. In his book *Awaken the Giant Within,* he talks a lot about gratitude and said that even if you do not feel grateful, you can always ask yourself, "What *could* I be grateful for?" I've found this to be a great mindset habit that works when you're stuck. A few years ago, when I had Ramit Sethi on my podcast, it struck me in the middle of the interview that I wanted to thank this person whom I looked up to and had learned so much from. (His *New York Times* best-selling book helped me get out of debt from the student loans I had. It was a major game changer in my life when I completed that.)

I don't know why, but saying that was hard. I guess I was worried it might come out weird. People wait their whole life to be acknowledged, and most of the time they only get it when they graduate from school or after it's too late and they are dead (this is the story of at least half of the famous impressionist painters whose priceless works hang in the world's most prestigious galleries). Why wait? I've realized. Every night I recount in my head what I am grateful for. My voice-mail message is about gratitude. And like I did with Ramit, I try to tell people in person how much they've done for me. In fact, you could say that this book is an exercise in gratitude, too!

Have a morning ritual. I learned the importance of a morning ritual from Tim Ferriss. He told me, "I think for entrepreneurs, it's very valuable for a week, for instance, to just figure out what your ritual is going to be in the morning or when you wake up. What is the first 60 minutes going to look like, and then script it out so that you do the same thing every day. I think it's a very freeing experience to allocate more thought power to the things that matter as opposed to trying to decide what you should have for breakfast today. I think ritual and routine are extremely important for people who want to be creative."

It doesn't have to be complicated. Here is my morning ritual on most days when I'm not traveling.

- Wake up and express to myself what I'm grateful for.
- Do a guided meditation for 10 minutes and visualize what I want to create in the world that day.
- Perform light stretching and simple yoga poses.
- Make my bed and brush my teeth.
- Work out for 30 to 60 minutes.
- Shower and get dressed.
- Have a green juice with my vitamins and breakfast.

Only then do I get into what I'm creating for the day with my business and vision.

Let go of reaction. Building a habit to let go, to not take anything personally, is a great way to reduce stress in your body. So when someone cuts you off on the highway, don't flip them off or curse or react in a negative way; instead, relax your body, take a deep breath, and focus on how safe you are and what you are most grateful for in the moment/day that is bigger than yourself and bigger than someone cutting you off.

Express your wants and needs. So many people shy away from expressing and communicating what they want and need (in life, relationships, business deals, and marriage; with their teammates, etc.). They bottle up their feelings and emotions, and it comes back to make them resentful or frustrated later. Of all the people in my life, my mom taught me this most clearly. She has always been big on open communication and being clear on what you want. Ask questions when you aren't sure about something instead of going along with it, and speak up to discuss what is on your mind even if you don't like confrontation.

Acknowledge others (and yourself). Similar to how I expressed my gratitude to Ramit, getting in the habit of acknowledging others is a powerful tool because our natural tendency is to deflect attention from the crowd. It's a defense mechanism. By acknowledging others—for their contribution, for their assistance, for their existence—you acknowledge their humanity and, in turn, your own. I saw the immediate impact and power of this habit in talking and working with Chris Lee. I watched him help others acknowledge those around them, and the change was almost instantaneous. This is incredibly important in the pursuit of greatness, because you will never get there alone. You need a team that will be your support system. The only way that team works is if you acknowledge each other for all the great things you do and are.

Be vulnerable. I also learned about the importance of being vulnerable and willing to discuss the past from Chris Lee, who showed me how to open up about some of the darkest moments in my childhood. He helped me share things I'd never told anyone before and exposed me to the freedom that resulted from that naked vulnerability. Not only is it a great virtue that helps build self-confidence, but getting in the habit of discussing the past instead of bottling it up is also the only way you will learn from your mistakes and grow as a person. Greatness is about getting better every day—at life, at business, at relationships, at whatever your vision is—and you can't do that if you keep making the same mistakes over and over again.

They say love is about the willingness to be completely vulnerable, but so is success in anything you do. Graham Holmberg doesn't become a CrossFit champion and Shawn Johnson doesn't become an Olympic champion unless they push themselves to the limit of their abilities and the brink of exhaustion—that is physical vulnerability. Angel Martinez doesn't help build Reebok into a footwear juggernaut without taking some serious risks in the early 1980s, just out of a recession, by going all in on an aerobics shoe—that is economic vulnerability.

This was one of the hardest habits for me to learn, because there is a lot from my past that for a long time I was trying to erase or forget or run away from. It's no coincidence that once I turned to face it and allowed myself to be vulnerable enough that I could talk about it openly with people that everything I was working toward started to take off!

I am not going to sit here and tell you that developing and practicing positive habits will be easy or fun all the time. It can be very hard, especially at the beginning. You'll have lapses, and that's okay. You just need to keep your eyes focused on your vision, harness your resolve to persevere against those temporary failures, and bust your butt like the champion you want to become. That is the price of greatness. Like Benjamin Franklin said, "Energy and persistence conquer all things." What I can tell you, however, is that slowly but surely you will begin to make strides and reap the rewards. And when that happens, you will embrace these positive habits with the same energy with which you are pursuing your own greatness.

EXERCISE #1:
The Attitude of Gratitude

As I mentioned in Chapter 2, by expressing gratitude in all areas of your life, you can fight internal and external adversity. If you concentrate on what you have, you'll always have more. If you concentrate on what you don't have, you'll never have enough. Cultivating positivity takes work. I'm not suggesting you can't ever have a bad day, but life is better if you develop an attitude of gratitude. Your homework for the next 2 weeks is simple and straightforward and, if done right, will begin to shift your entire perspective on how you interact with everyone in your life. For the past year, I have made it a habit to tell whomever I'm with at the end of my day the three things I'm grateful for. It's awesome.

By doing this every day, you'll consciously begin looking for things to be grateful for. You'll feel more alive and receptive to the goodness that comes in your life, and you'll increase your joy of simple moments.

Some things that you might want to express gratitude for:

- Catching up with a friend you haven't spoken to in a while
- The great workout you had this morning
- Landing a new client and booking the gig
- Completing any project you were working on
- The love you received today

No matter how bad your day is, there is so much to be appreciated. The fact that you are alive and have been given another day is a huge gift. We have so much to be grateful for, including the essentials and basics—the food we eat, our environment, our health, our friends.

Share your gratitude and give it away. This is something you should do when things are going well in your life *and* when everything seems to be against you.

These small things might feel completely irrelevant and trivial in comparison to your goals or your vision, and I understand that, but what you need to understand is that the effects these small things have on your life bleed into all areas—not just one.

EXERCISE #2:
Write Your Habits Manifesto

This is straight from the Gretchen Rubin playbook of building good habits. She published her own Habits Manifesto in 2014.

HABITS MANIFESTO

What we do *every day* matters more than what we do *once in a while.*

Make it easy to do right and hard to go wrong.

Focus on actions, not outcomes.

By giving something up, we may gain.

Things often get harder before they get easier.

When we give more to ourselves, we can ask more from ourselves.

We're not very different from other people, but those differences are *very* important.

It's easier to change our surroundings than ourselves.

We can't make people change, but when we change, others may change.

We should make sure the things we do to feel *better* don't make us feel *worse.*

We manage what we monitor.

Once we're ready to begin, begin *now.*

Contemplate the dozen statements Gretchen makes. Think about each of them as they relate to your life. How do they apply? What would you add or take away or change? Why?

Now look back to page 162 at the lists of positive habits I compiled for myself and the wealthiest people in the
world. Make a checklist to see if you are doing any of
them or if you are doing the opposite.

Then look for three things on those lists that you can
add to your daily routine for the next 2 weeks, and start
applying them right now. It almost doesn't matter which
three you choose to start. After the 2 weeks, assess
where you are in your life, how you are feeling, and if you
see the value in these habits.

After those 2 weeks, add three more habits to your
routine and adjust the others to support your vision until
you are on track to living a life full of positive habits. I'm
not perfect and I don't always have my habits in check, so I
don't expect you to either. But when you set a foundation
of positive habits, the rewards that manifest down the
line are almost always far better than you can imagine.
And they get you that much closer to achieving your vision
and that much farther down the path toward greatness.

EXERCISE #3:
The 28-Day Morning Routine Challenge

Small changes lead to big shifts. What you do when you
wake up sets your pace for the day. And while goal setting, vision casting, and the power of intention are all
extremely important, greatness is about taking action
toward change.

This month your challenge is a *daily morning* challenge.

This exercise will be like setting the refresh button on how you begin each day. The 28-day challenge is long enough to reset a bad habit and propel you into greatness. Completing this challenge will make you more efficient and focused with your time. Your time is valuable, and I want you to attack this challenge as intentionally as you can with how you spend it.

For the next 4 weeks, you're committing to an action you will be taking on this month to work toward your vision. This challenge is forcing you to break through and commit to the simple (and possibly mundane) tasks that will help you lead a life of greatness.

Choose from one of the following to do every morning before you check your e-mail or phone or do any work.

- Spend 30 minutes writing as soon as you wake up (journaling your goals, free writing from your heart, writing about your vision/struggles/dream).
- Make your bed—this is something I do every morning, as it gives me a sense of completion early in the day.
- Make a to-do list for the day. Create a list of your top priorities or the most important things you need to accomplish that day.
- Work out, stretch, or go on a walk to get up and moving first thing in the morning before distractions get in the way.
- Sit down and eat breakfast. This may seem simple, but instead of grabbing the coffee and bagel to go/ in your car and eating mindlessly, set time before you leave in the morning to prepare and enjoy a healthy, balanced breakfast.

The decision of what to do in the morning is your own, but make it something that, even in a small way, supports your bigger vision. Establishing a morning routine sets the tone for the rest of the day—so select one that can propel you forward in achieving your dreams.

COACHING TIP

It is absolutely critical that you weigh the price and the reward for the decisions you make on a daily basis. And don't kid yourself—everything has a price and a reward. There is a reward for good habits (growth), and there is a reward for bad ones (instant gratification). Unfortunately, the prices for each are way out of whack. And oftentimes, the price can be your ultimate vision. You need to figure out which habits give you the best chance of reaching your goals.

It's time to get connected to your vision, understand its power, and realize that it's not worth the instant gratification that bad habits pay out to you. Because when you put positive habits in place, you set yourself up to win. Period. When you don't have them in place, something almost always falls out of order in your life and you will likely not know why. It's time to step up and get serious with your daily actions, as this is what builds the momentum in your life toward the vision you want to achieve.

GET GROUNDED

Having played sports my entire life, I know the importance of playing with a powerful team and what kind of team to look for when your goal is greatness. With every season in sports and in life, there will always be a different role that we play or that others around us play. Sometimes we'll be the star, and other times we'll need to take a supportive role. We must learn to flow with the changes as we grow and bring on new opportunities and experiences in life. I used to try to do everything on my own when people would "let me down," and I thought I'd go through life solo proving others wrong. That ended up emotionally draining me and was stressful beyond belief (not to mention very lonely). It wasn't until I began allowing others to support my dreams and me that life started to come to me with ease.

If you've been playing solo in your life, I want you to open up to the possibility of what a team could look like moving forward. That might require you to adjust your attitude and mindset or find a whole new team altogether. Let's dive in here and see what comes up for you with my exercises at the end of this chapter.

CHAPTER 7

BUILD A
WINNING TEAM

"If you want to go fast, go alone;
if you want to go far, go together."'
—**African proverb**

Justin Bieber has sold millions of records, toured hundreds of cities, performed in front of thousands of people, and personally made hundreds of millions of dollars in a handful of years. If you sat down and asked him how this could have happened, how he could have gone from uploading little videos of himself singing on YouTube to being one of the biggest stars in the history of music, he would give you a single name: Scooter Braun.

That is the hugely successful talent manager who discovered Bieber from a YouTube video when the megastar was only 14 years old and living in Canada. At just 34 years old—still a kid himself by some people's standards—Scooter emerged as one of the music industry's most influential and intelligent people for one reason: He knew how to build a winning team. It's not just about finding talented individuals (creative, management, or otherwise), he realized. The path to platinum status and personal greatness is about turning those people into a team. It's a lesson understood by leading figures across disciplines; their experience—as well as my own—shows that greatness simply cannot be achieved in a vacuum or through a solitary effort.

Scooter learned this invaluable lesson from an unlikely and unwitting mentor: legendary NBA coach Phil Jackson. As a kid, Scooter wanted to be a basketball player. And like most kids, at some point he realized he wasn't tall enough. It usually happens when you're pretending to be Michael Jordan, down by two, with the clock winding down, and then someone who seems the size of Shaquille O'Neal eats your lunch. When that moment occurs, some kids hang up their kicks while others channel their love of the sport in a different direction. In Scooter's case, he picked up Phil Jackson's classic book, *Sacred Hoops.* By the time he closed the back cover, he had decided he wanted to be a coach. It was there that he fell in love with the idea of creating the perfect winning team.

CULTIVATE STRONG RELATIONSHIPS

Scooter built his first real-life team in college as a nightclub promoter. He learned early on that cultivating strong relationships in business and in life is a basic building block for greatness. Which is why today, if you spent some time in the offices of Scooter's company, SB Projects— considered to be one of the most important music firms in the business—you'd see a team made up of his best friends and contacts, some dating back to high school.

Talking to Scooter about the intersection of his personal and professional relationships made me realize just how important my own relationships have been on my journey toward greatness—particularly in business and sports. With sports, I've been on great teams and awful ones. I've also been on great teams that lost and awful teams that won. But it was the ones that were so toxic and disconnected that I literally wanted to quit (and sometimes did) that had the greatest impact.

I remember my freshman year at Southwest Minnesota State playing for a coach whose style of leadership resembled a potent mix of Bobby Knight and the drill sergeant from *Full Metal Jacket.* If you did something wrong, he got up and screamed in your face. If you didn't do something fast enough, he took great pains (and pleasure) in calling you out in front of everyone—humiliating you. There is nothing worse than being on a team with that kind of negative energy. It brings everyone else down. It's not like we wanted to fail. We all wanted to win. We all wanted to succeed and do our best. It was our coach's belief that the best way to do that wasn't to build relationships with his team and create unstoppable winning chemistry but instead to scare us to victory by making us more afraid of losing than excited about winning.

Needless to say, his leadership style didn't work for me nor for many of my teammates. Our team never really gelled. We looked ahead to each game on the schedule not as an opportunity to get better but as 1 week closer to the end of this miserable experience. But that team, miserable though it may have been, taught me one of the most valuable lessons I've learned: You need to get everyone rowing in the same direction, and the only way you do this effectively is by cultivating the kinds of strong relationships where heading in the same direction feels like the only option. And that direction can't be as far away from you as they can possibly get either: At best, you will go nowhere. What's more likely is that their numbers will overwhelm your singular force of will, and you'll head in the wrong direction.

This phenomenon is especially true in dysfunctional workplaces and families. Many of us have suffered in jobs where you are on edge every day, waiting for your boss to yell at you or call out your mistakes in front of everyone, never acknowledging you for the hard work you put in day in and day out. At home, with parents always yelling at each other (or at you), never feeling like your talents are being nurtured or cultivated, all you can do is put your head down and simply do your best to survive without getting punished.

The best companies and families are great teams. The importance of building winning teams and the principles that go into them aren't just about sports, they're about all areas of life, all of the time.

SURROUND YOURSELF WITH GREATNESS

Building a powerful team is obviously important, but how do you know the difference between a good team and a bad one? How do you make sure that you have a winning team behind you or, even better, feel like you are just one player on a team that is changing the world together?

These were questions I was not equipped to answer on my own. This was probably the main reason I decided to start (and attend) the School of Greatness, so I could connect a collection of professors and teachers to my own winning team and join them in the great things they were doing.

Don Yaeger is the author of seven best-selling books and is best known for his collaborations with Hall of Fame running back Walter Payton and another famed basketball coach, John Wooden. The most important lesson Coach Wooden ever taught Don was this: You will never outperform your inner circle. If you want to achieve outer success, improve your inner circle.

This is what Don passed on to me in my time with him. Our capacity for success and greatness is embodied by the people we surround ourselves with. If you aspire to greatness, make sure that you have greatness around you. For Don, this was an eye-opening insight that applied not only to basketball and his projects with John and other athletes but also to life in general.

"I find myself, all the time, thinking about my inner circle," Don admitted. "Who's in it? Who should be in it? Whether or not some people maybe need to have a different spot in the circle."

The difficulty lies in the fact that some people who have been in your circle for years, often by default, can't simply be cut off. Don was talking specifically about family members.

"Let's be honest, you can't get rid of a family member, right? So what I realized was rather than the amount of time I was allotting every week to conversation, maybe it's half that. It really is a great challenge, but governing who you put in your circle is one of those places where your decision making will impact you greatly."

Now here's the million-dollar question you need to ask yourself. It's a question Don asked me, and I'm sure Coach Wooden asked him numerous times over their 12 years working together: How is this model for greatness different when we're talking about sports as opposed to business or relationships or life? The answer, of course, is that it's not.

Think about it: A successful book (as I hope this one will be) requires the right editors, the right publisher, the right publicists, the right designers, the right researchers, and the right support staff—all of whom will make you better, none of whom will waste your time. Without excellence in each of those areas, it is impossible to have an excellent and successful book. Don has hit the *New York Times* nonfiction bestseller list seven times. According to him, there are fewer than 50 individuals to ever accomplish that. Don didn't do this alone; he did it with the help of his team.

As transformative as this insight was for Don—after collaborating with Coach Wooden, Don's focus shifted toward mentorship and greatness and the notion of "paying it forward"—it was equally so for me, if only a little different. I'd heard before how you are the average of the five people you spend the most time with, for better or worse. But that advice was related to happiness and self-improvement. I'd never heard it like this, in relation to teams and to success and greatness. Then Don hit me with another John Wooden quote: "You show me your friends, and I'll show you your future."

That brought it home for me and the entire purpose behind the School of Greatness. Think about Rich Roll and his wife, Julie Piatt, who was the one who bought him the bike that changed his life. She was the catalyst and inspiration for him to get back to working out and change his entire health lifestyle. Or Kyle Maynard and Shawn Johnson, whose parents supported and facilitated their passions—from football and wrestling to ballet and gymnastics. Or Angel Martinez and the elderly relatives who took him in and gave him the opportunity to have and pursue the American dream.

Each of these great men and women had friends and family who pushed them to be greater, who ensured that they would have a world-changing future. Beware of people who instead will drag you down or make you feel bad for having ambition. Sometimes it's hard to be honest with yourself about relationships like that when you're focused on achieving your vision and living your dream. But it's important to take a step back every once in a while and look at your inner circle. Are they pushing you to be great? Are they supporting your dream? Because that's what a winning team does, that's what it looks like, and that's why you need to have one.

FIND THE RIGHT MENTOR(S)

Let's say you are one of those people who has to rebuild your inner circle, and you're trying to figure out the first person to add to your winning team. Who is it? It's the coach. Your mentor. Your advisor. Your father/mother figure. Their role on your path to greatness is literally invaluable.

The writer Denis Waitley has an apt analogy that I'd like to borrow and paraphrase here, from an article titled "The Champion Within" from his very popular newsletter.

He uses an example relating new military technology to mentors. A missile system that was introduced during the Gulf War in 1991 was revolutionary because it would self-adjust its trajectory to ensure that it kept its target in range. Likewise, as Denis says, "A highly motivated person, when he or she has targeted a worthwhile goal, uses a coach or mentor the same way a missile uses the new guidance system—to assist you in making adjustments and navigating difficult, uncertain, ever-changing terrain."

Without the right mentor, we're like an unguided missile on the path to greatness. If we're lucky, we'll end up exactly where we need to go. But that's only if everything goes precisely as planned. Life never seems to happen that way, though—especially when we're trying to do something different, something more. What we need is someone who can not only help us set our original course but also constantly correct and guide us through the problems and adversity we will inevitably face.

This brings us back to Scooter. His first mentor was Jermaine Dupri, a successful record producer, songwriter, and rapper, whom he met while promoting parties and eventually ended up working for. Dupri taught him the music business and how to work with artists. But Scooter didn't stop there. "Sometimes people say they have one mentor. I've never had one mentor," he told me. "If I had one mentor, it'd be my father, but I have other really great mentors as well: people like Jeffrey Katzenberg and Lucian Grainge, who's the chairman of Universal Music Group. We're very close, and he's been an incredible mentor and friend. David Geffen has become a mentor to me as well. Those kinds of people I'm eternally grateful to because they allow me to draw from them."

When Scooter reached out to Justin Bieber and sketched out a path for the young singer's career, it was these ideas that he founded it on. Without the right friends, without the right guidance, without the right team (along with all the hard work and talent he had), there was no way that Bieber would break through. We are so heavily influenced by the people we spend the most time with that we can't afford to leave it up to chance. Being selective about mentors, friends, and partners is going to be one of the biggest factors in the journey to greatness.

Point being, it's extremely important—I'd even say absolutely necessary—to find the right coaches for you if you want to achieve greatness in any area of your life. Can you be successful without them? Of course. But the greatest athletes in the world all have coaches even when they are at the peak of their game. In fact, they want coaching and feedback on ways to get better and improve more than anyone. Michael Jordan didn't add all those new moves in the off-season or win all those championships in the postseason without Phil Jackson on the bench. It's important to find coaches who inspire you but also give it to you straight. Ones you can look up to and take their guidance seriously. Ones you can commit to and show that you are willing to take action to achieve your own greatness.

THE POWER OF POSITIVE ENERGY

"I've been able to bring some amazing people into my life and surround myself with people, I think, who are skilled in ways that I am not, and we've been able to scale an incredible business because they make things happen," Scooter said. It's something he teaches his artists, too. They can't do it alone. They can't be successful in isolation. But Scooter looks for something else in addition to talent and smarts: positivity.

"I'm a firm believer that it's more important to have positive energy around you than the smartest people. Now, luckily I've been able to have, in my opinion, some of the smartest people around me who are also positive," he told me. I've found this in my own business. I'd rather have someone who has a tremendous amount of heart and hustle over the most talented person who has an energy of entitlement about them and selfish tendencies.

This is the tricky part about talent within a team: It is a delicate balancing act between the positivity of heart and hustle and the negativity that can arise with the natural competitiveness that develops within teams. Smart, talented people want to achieve. They want to realize the potential that so many—including the person who has hired them—have identified in them. The key is to show them, by example, how everyone individually wins when the team wins. If you allow ego to get in the way, the positive energy you could otherwise harness and direct outward at the competition or the marketplace morphs into negative energy and turns inward. You end up with people competing against each other, or worse, against you, and the vision you have built for your business and your life. Defining precisely what success looks like is a big part of turning the natural competitive instincts of smart, talented, ambitious people into positive, supportive energy instead of negative, destructive, selfish energy.

You see this in sports teams as well, where a team of "average" players can beat a team of All-Stars if they work together, are positive, and stick to the game plan. The way they win is by passing the ball and working within the system, not trying to do too much by themselves. Instead, they understand that everyone has their role, and they stick to that role. If everyone does their own job and doesn't try to win the game alone, then they give themselves a chance to win. After all, you can't hit a game-winning grand slam until you have players on base.

"I learned that lesson the hard way," Scooter admitted to me. "I had some negativity in my life before, and you start to question yourself because negativity projects onto you. You start to look in the mirror and say, 'Am I really a good person? Am I doing the right thing?' That isn't you. That's their bullshit feeding on you." You've got to have positive energy to create winning chemistry. It's that simple.

It reminds me of a quote by Edmund Lee, who encouraged people to "surround yourself with the dreamers and the doers, the believers and the thinkers, but most of all, surround yourself with those who seek greatness within you even when you don't see it yourself."

Beyond surrounding yourself with these positive people, it's also important that you build a network of them. Bill Clinton, in his rise from a broken home to the governorship of Arkansas to the presidency, created a network of some 10,000 physical note cards containing the names, addresses, and relationship history of classmates, professors, friends, lawyers, donors, supporters, reporters, and influencers that he could cultivate and call on when needed. He became not just a connector, as Malcolm Gladwell described and I tried to emulate on

LinkedIn, but a *superconnector*—working every room, schmoozing every influencer, charming every guest. Eventually, he digitized this system and continues to use it to this day for his work with the Clinton Foundation. He is living proof that, as my friend and networking expert Porter Gale puts it, "your network is your *net worth*."

PUTTING IT ALL TOGETHER

But not every talented and positive team wins, as we know. There is more to greatness than that. It takes strategy and leadership. This was something I also asked Scooter about. How do you ensure that you get the most out of your team?

"You've got to realize," he told me, "the only way to scale is to delegate and to empower others and to say, 'You know what? They're not going to do it exactly like me, but they're going to do it exactly like them.'" You have to be okay with the fact that some people will be better than you at certain things in the long run. Why should that threaten you? Isn't that why you brought them on in the first place? There is always friction on any team. With a bench player picking up the starting job (which means kicking someone else to the bench), with new hires, as people get raises and increase their "rank" in companies, there will always be competition and egos that come out.

Being transparent in the beginning about the importance of communication and clearing up any misunderstandings with people so no one holds on to frustration is an essential part of a winning team. The "clearing" process, or open communication, will allow the team to have break-throughs in stressful situations instead of breakdowns and implosion.

Scooter brought the analogy home to me after we played a pickup basketball game together: "That's the same idea as when we play basketball. Sometimes you're going to make a great assist and a guy's going to miss that easy shot, and you're going to be frustrated because that was another assist on your stat line. But at the end of the day, it isn't about our individual stat line, it's about winning the game." The key, even if the missed gimme layup was the difference between victory and defeat, is to communicate with your teammate about what happened. Like we talked about in Chapter 6, you need to let go of reaction and get on the same page about what went wrong and what went right, so you can go back out there tomorrow and do it all over again, together. After all, as Scooter reminded me, "you cannot win the game on your own."

Jack Welch, former CEO and chairman of General Electric, who knows a thing or two about building a winning team, has written things on this subject that very much apply to what Scooter was talking about. In an article for *Newsweek* a few years ago, he and his wife, Suzy Welch, wrote, "First, the leaders of winning teams always—always—let their people know where they stand... Second, winning teams know the game plan." It's your job, as you assemble your team, to let them know what's important and create a plan for them to follow. Not a plan that's all about you. Instead, it's about creating a plan in which everyone has a role and everyone's role is designed for them to thrive in. That's what Scooter has done so well.

THE TEAM ISN'T JUST ABOUT THE BUSINESS

There is one final thing I think is worth discussing here, especially as Scooter's most prominent protégé has had no shortage of troubles at various points in his life. Justin Bieber has been arrested for DUI and drag racing in Miami; he's been taken in for egging a neighbor's house in Calabasas, California; he's been charged with hitting a limo driver in Toronto; he tagged a hotel wall in Brazil and ran through customs and passport control in Turkey. Yet Scooter stood by him. Perhaps because he knows that all young people, especially famous young people, do dumb things. But I think there is another reason. Scooter doesn't see what he does as being just business. His clients and his employees are his family. And family is everything.

I realized that when I spotted some writing on Scooter's wrist. It was a tattoo. Just one word: *Family*. When I asked him about his family, he lit up. His grandparents were Holocaust survivors. His brother, Adam, whom you'll meet next chapter, is an amazing person doing incredible things. And his parents? The day I interviewed him for the podcast just happened to be his parents' 35th wedding anniversary.

> To have parents who really, truly love each other and are good to each other, and to witness that growing up and to have that love all the time, I always felt full. I always felt safe.

Yet for a period in his late teens and early twenties, Scooter lost sight of that love. He still appreciated it for what it was but not for its role in guiding his life.

"I was lost, and I was chasing the money because I didn't really understand. I was just going for it. What I realized was all I'm doing it for is this," he said as he pointed to the tattoo. Interestingly, he talked about getting that tattoo for a while before going in to get it inked. What finally pushed him to go in and make it real?

The day before, Jay Williams, the former All-American point guard from Duke and the second overall pick in the 2002 NBA Draft by the Chicago Bulls, had gotten into a motorcycle accident that would ultimately end his professional basketball career. "Jay's one of my closest friends," Scooter said. "I had chickened out about getting this tattoo a couple weeks earlier, and when I found out what happened to him, I realized I couldn't take that for granted anymore."

Add to the mix the fact that his mother had fallen ill during that period—she's fine now, thank goodness—and you can see the power and meaning this tattoo carries for Scooter.

"For the rest of my life, people will ask me about this tattoo," he told me, "and I will have to tell this story of why I got it, which is this simple, and it will remind me for the rest of my life what's really important."

But how can work and family be the same? Much like Don Yaeger talked about, you can't fire someone from being related to you. Okay, so it's not a perfect analogy, but it is important. When I first started my company and I hired people, I used to think that they were there to work *for* me. That almost always ended badly because I set myself and them up to lose. I've since learned that I am actually in service to my team, as well as to everyone else. Just like you are to your family—it's a matter of give and take, mutual respect, and, ultimately, gratitude and love.

What I try to think about after learning about great teams from Scooter and Don Yaeger is this: How can I be of service to every member of my team and set them up to win as best as possible? This doesn't mean I need to hold everyone's hand daily or coddle them; it simply means that I make sure that if anyone ever needs to talk about anything, I'm always there to listen, and that they are set up with what they need to be successful in their position and their role.

Together we win *as a team*. Not just me, not just a paycheck for them, but a winning team, aiming for and achieving greatness.

EXERCISE #1:
Take Inventory of Your Relationships

It's not always easy to find quality people to be on your team. You might go through some disappointing relationships before you find the right people, but don't compromise. If you let a few difficult experiences convince you to go it alone, you'll hamstring yourself. I look back on my career-ending injury, and I had many mentors during that time, but I specifically attribute my transition into business to one man who I am forever grateful to have met—Chris Hawker. Chris was a successful inventor and could have easily brushed me aside when I so eagerly requested to work with him. Instead, I showed him the value I could bring, so he took me under his wing and shared his wisdom and experience with me. Think about the people you most look up to versus the people you spend the most time with. If those lists are drastically different, fix that. Reach out to your role models and mentors and involve them in your journey. Cut out those people you spend a lot of time with who are not helping you on your path to greatness.

To find out if someone is serving you in your life or holding you back, ask yourself these four questions.

1. Do I feel energized or stressed when I'm around or think about this person?
2. Does this person inspire me or have a negative mindset around me?
3. Does this person pursue greatness in their life, or are they often a victim to circumstances?
4. Do they get excited about my success and want to see me succeed, or do they complain about their own life when I achieve my dreams?

If your answers left you on the positive side, then it sounds like this person is still a great team member in your life! If they are on the energy-draining side, however, you may want to have a "clearing conversation" with them and let them know how you feel about your relationship. Come from a loving place when you talk to them about this and don't fault them for anything. Then make your request for how you'd like to be in relationship moving forward and what you can expect from them moving forward.

EXAMPLES OF CLEARING CONVERSATIONS

Hi, (friend/colleague). I appreciate the time we share together. I have created a new vision for my life, and I am making a commitment to being more positive. I feel like the conversations we tend to have are negative and not productive, and I take responsibility for this. Are you open to working on this with me?

> Hi, (parent/spouse/friend). I love you and appreciate you. I
> have taken a stand in my life to work on my goals and not
> fixate on the stress in life. I want to focus my energy on what
> I'm grateful for and not complain about what I do not have.
> Do you support me and stand to keep me to my word?

Most relationships don't work because people don't clearly communicate their requests in a loving way; it usually comes in the form of an attack, which rarely solves anything. You don't need to tell them where they are not supporting, but let them choose to support you in the way you need. This is the path of least confrontation. If you are like me, you want to get clear with all your friends, colleagues, and family in the most direct yet least aggressive way possible.

> Hi, (parent/colleague/friend). I want to start by saying I
> appreciate you, and I request of you . . .

> Hi, (boyfriend/girlfriend/significant other). I care about your
> vision, but you seem to be off course and you are also
> steering me off course by . . . Let's commit ourselves to . . .

If the relationship doesn't shift over a specific period of time that you define with the person you are trying to get clear with, and you continue to need to make that request, then it's another sign that you may want to distance yourself from the person and start surrounding yourself with a more positive inner circle for your team.

Always try to take action together, but if extreme measures need to be taken, that is when the power of *no* comes into play. It takes strength to remove someone from your life or take a step back from that person's energy. Understand that nothing is more important than your emotional well-being. This drain will undoubtedly hold you back from greatness. This exercise is a game changer.

EXERCISE #2:
Join or Create a Mastermind

A mastermind is a group of influential individuals who support you to take your business or life to the next level. With the collective mind of the group, you find support, information, and resources to serve you on your path. And you will get there much faster than trying to do it on your own.

I was just starting out in my business when I joined my first mastermind with an online marketing group. It was essentially a 2-day meeting where we sat at a round table with a group of 15 other online marketing business professionals and shared best practices and ideas and supported each other on our specific goals. The power of the mastermind lies with the people in it and the opportunities you can create from that network. In this first meeting, I ended up sitting next to someone who directly helped me make $250,000 over the next 3 months by selling my products as an affiliate partner and referring me to five others who promoted my product as well. This was a huge boost to everything we were doing at the time, accelerating our profits and success much faster than we ever could have without the mastermind.

Masterminds were the key ingredient for me in taking my business from six figures to seven figures so quickly. There is no other way it would have grown that quickly. It's essential to be a part of at least one mastermind (if not more), and I highly recommend being the creator and leader of one yourself at some point, too.

Napoleon Hill, the legendary author of *Think and Grow Rich*, has a great way to think about masterminds: "the coordination of knowledge and effort of two or more people, who work toward a definite purpose, in the spirit of harmony." This isn't actually his description of mastermind groups—it's really one of his main principles for how to become successful. The fact that those two concepts overlap so fully—masterminds and being successful—is not a coincidence in my mind.

If you're still not sold, or if someone has given you a negative impression of masterminds, let me try to clear things up for you. Here is what masterminds are or can be.

- Teams of influencers in your community connected for a purpose
- A catalyst for business and personal growth
- A space for goals and holding each other accountable
- A peer advisory board
- An education, support, and brainstorming group
- Confidential
- A commitment
- A group of people supporting each other to create the life/business they want

- Supportive of your success
- A group of people who have your best interest in mind

Here is what masterminds are not or should never be.

- Group therapy

Masterminds are meant to help you attain your major purpose in life by borrowing the wisdom and using the education, experience, and influence of other people who are mutually invested in your success. When run right, they allow you to accomplish in the next 6 to 12 months more than you could accomplish without them in your entire life if you depended solely upon yourself.

There are two essential components to every successful mastermind group: the right attitude and the right members. You can have one without the other and get by okay, but we're not interested in that. We're not interested in settling. This book is not called *The School of Average*. It's about greatness, so that's what we're going to strive for: a great mastermind, with a great attitude and great members.

The mastermind attitude looks like this. You are:

- Friendly and cooperative
- Noncompetitive
- Willing to be creative and brainstorm ideas/ solutions for others' businesses
- Supportive of each other with total honesty, respect, and compassion
- Not ever, at any point, indifferent

Think of your mastermind as your basketball dream team. It is a group of differently yet equally talented peers who are there to support your success. Thus, selecting members for your own mastermind group should look like this. They should have:

- A strong commitment to the group
- Similar success and experience
- An agreement about the mastermind attitude
- An agreement on written guidelines created by and for the group
- The ability to give and take equally when it comes to advice, support, and resources

Ultimately, your mastermind group should start with 4 to 6 people (up to 15 max) and a simple (no more than one page) mastermind agreement you're all aligned with that includes:

- The group name
- How you're going to connect (in person or via Skype, GoToMeeting, Google Hangouts, or phone)
- How long your meetings will be (1 to 2 hours minimum is recommended, but some could be 2 or 3 days)
- How often you will meet (weekly, monthly, quarterly, etc.)
- When you will meet
- The agenda for your meetings

Understand all this about masterminds and follow this process with purpose and intentionality, and you are on your way to building a winning team for your business and your life. For more information on this and the different masterminds to join, go to schoolofgreatness.com/resources.

EXERCISE #3:
The Three Lists to Freedom

This exercise I learned from my friend and "Virtual CEO" Chris Ducker. Chris is the author of *Virtual Freedom,* a book that teaches people how to work with virtual staff in order to have more time for themselves while at the same time being more productive. This was specifically designed for businesspeople but is easily adapted to use in your life. It will fundamentally change how you manage both life and business.

Get a piece of paper and a pen. Create three columns with the following headlines:

- Things you don't like doing
- Things you can't do
- Things you shouldn't do

Now fill in all the things that fit in these categories relating to your business or your lifestyle.

The Things You Don't Like Doing

These are the things you procrastinate on all day. Things like replying to social media messages, managing e-mail, doing your bookkeeping, etc. Life and business demand that you get these things done, so it's your job to find someone you can pass them off to or develop a system that allows you to be more efficient.

The Things You Can't Do

Many people, especially entrepreneurs, feel like they have to do a lot of things themselves. The only problem is, there are many things you can't do even if you wanted to. I love design and playing with designs on my computer, but I'm the worst at using design software and designing things myself. After a few hours of intense work, the best I can draw is a bad-looking stick figure of a cat! Just because you have an interest in something or doing it yourself would be cheaper doesn't mean you are qualified to do it at a high level. In fact, your lack of experience and expertise might actually make doing it yourself more costly than hiring a professional, since it would take up more of your valuable time that could otherwise be spent on high-level business and life activities that you're actually good at.

The Things You Shouldn't Do

In my business, I'm very capable of doing a number of different things that I shouldn't be doing even though I like doing some of them. That's just the natural consequence of earning five-figure consulting and speaking fees for a couple hours of my time. It means I shouldn't be spending 15 minutes figuring out what to post on social media or handling customer support. I may be good at those things or like doing them, but they are literally a waste of my time.

Chris Ducker still prepares these lists every 90 days because, he says, we sometimes slip back into bad habits out of necessity or we just get busy with life. I recommend checking in with this as well to see what tasks you can put in these lists and start letting go of them.

DON'T LIKE DOING	CAN'T DO	SHOULDN'T DO
Checking e-mail	Graphic design	Updating social media
Managing my calendar	Developing a Web site	Handling customer support
Handling basic inquiries	Editing podcast episodes	Managing company blog
Researching travel	Bookkeeping and accounts	Collecting dry cleaning

This becomes the road map to working with your team. These lists flag the jobs that aren't the best uses of your time with the skills you have for making a bigger impact and getting closer to your vision. They indicate how to best set up your team or support structure.

When I first started in business, I worked 15-hour days because I did all of these tasks on my own. I wasn't good at a lot of them, which meant they took me even longer. When I switched my mentality and allowed others to support me and join my team, the stress went away, efficiency went up, and I was able to focus on what I loved doing at all times instead of the things I didn't need to do. My life seemed to come together and flow. It's been like living in a dream world ever since, and it's possible for anyone who is committed to making it happen as well!

Keep in mind that this exercise isn't just for entrepreneurs or for businesses generally. It works as well in your personal life. I hate shopping and get tired in about 30 minutes at the mall, I struggle with cooking (I enjoy doing it, but it rarely tastes as good as it should), and I shouldn't be doing yard work or deep cleaning my place. Based on the time I use in my business and toward making money that I charge for speaking, coaching, or consulting, my time is better spent doing what I'm great at and hiring others on my team for support with those lists as well.

Think of all the things in your personal life that you want to add to this. Even if you don't think you can afford to hire or outsource for some of these tasks, put them on the list anyway. There are tools and apps coming online every day designed to solve these problems and offer support on a friendly budget.

EXERCISE # 4:
The Personality Matrix

The Personality Matrix is a process you can follow to discover not only who you are but also to understand whom you are interacting with on a daily basis. Imagine knowing exactly what to say to someone—a teammate, a family member, a business colleague, a customer—because you know their personality type. Imagine being able to immediately connect with them in a way they understand and relate to. There are a number of personality tests online and different ways of examining them, but I

learned about this process from Chris Lee, so it has stuck
with me to great success. The Personality Matrix divides
people into four main personality styles: promoters, analyzers, controllers, and supporters.

The Promoter (Opposite of an Analyzer)

The gift of a promoter is the ability to contribute and
grow many ideas. Their primary challenge is with completing projects. They are the life of the party and have a
lot of passion but, because of this challenge, tend to break
their word and become overwhelmed.

If you find yourself in the position of trying to sell
something to a promoter or get them excited about an
idea of yours, there's one reliable way to do it: Show up
excited. Be enthusiastic. Talk about your experience and
how great it will make them feel.

Promoters are relationship driven, all about fun and
energy.

The Analyzer (Opposite of a Promoter)

The gift of an analyzer is that they are detail oriented,
disciplined, systematic, process driven, structured, and
organized.

If you're selling to an analyzer, you must know everything about what you're working with down to the small-
est details.

Analyzers are their word. When an analyzer says
they will do something, you can take it to the bank. They
lack passion and spontaneity, and they can show up as if

they are hardly alive. Analyzers are visual and logical. They are formal in their dress and their energy.

The Controller (Opposite of a Supporter)

The gift of a controller is that they can get things done. They are driven, decisive, confident, goal oriented, and focused.

When you're selling to a controller, you better show up powerfully and dressed well. Agree with them and speak in a leading way that implies that they believe your idea was theirs. Stroke their ego. Connect with them at their level.

Controllers appear insensitive, mean, uncaring, and inflexible, and they pay for it in their personal and business relationships. A controller is dominant and formal. You have to present to them in a dominant, formal way.

The Supporter (Opposite of a Controller)

The gift of a supporter is being a giver focused on emotions, love, acknowledgment, and self-respect.

Selling to a supporter is all about emotion. Discuss the benefits not just to those who would be customers or users but also to everyone around who stands to be better off due to the actions or decisions you're proposing.

Supporters often come off like doormats. They don't stand up for themselves immediately, and it may seem like you're taking advantage of them. The way to avoid that is to provide positive feedback, which they respond to overwhelmingly.

So, which one are you? What is your dominant personality and your secondary personality? Being a leader in relationships requires the ability to access and be flexible with each of these personality types at any given time. If you can match or complement the energy of others around you, you can understand them better, and they will in turn feel more appreciated. Most important, being a successful, productive member of a good team demands that you don't tip too far in any one direction.

Are you an analyzer? Be outrageous!

A controller? Be vulnerable.

A promoter? Keep your word.

A supporter? Tell yourself, "I matter."

COACHING TIP

We are all in this together, and it's time to start living in a world where you embrace this concept. Life flows when you find a team you gel with, so why not start finding the All-Star players right now? The way you do this is by first becoming an All-Star player yourself. Do the work, improve your attitude, hustle, and sharpen your skills so that everyone else wants to make you a starter on their team! When you become a valuable asset to the world, then the world starts giving you what you dream of. It's that simple.

People matter. And you can't achieve anything great on your own. Letting people know how much they matter and how much you care about them is equally important (if not more). The saying goes that "people don't care about how much you know until they know how much you care." This is true in family, sports, business, and any other situation in life. Continue to surround yourself with positive people who care about you and always find ways to create a win-win in every relationship in your life. Relationships are the key to success, and it's time to start investing in yours.

GET GROUNDED

For many years, I thought there had to be a winner and a loser in sports, business, and life. I was so attached to the scoreboard and making sure that my team and I had more points than our opponent that I failed for a long time to grasp the meaning of a full life: creating win-win relationships. I never thought about what happens when you do "win." Then what? Are you just supposed to keep winning and gaining momentum and building an empire of success, yet be the loneliest winner in the world? Or is there more to living a great life?

Slowly but surely, moments happened where I witnessed and started to understand the value of giving back and being in service to others. This may be my most important lesson to date. Making money matters, having your needs met matters, achieving your vision matters, and turning your dreams into reality matters. But if you aren't looking for ways to improve the lives of everyone around you—your family, community, environment, and the world—then what's the point of all of it? In this chapter, we dissect the value of giving back. It's not about looking good or doing it because you feel you are supposed to. I want you to really see why giving to others is so important, because it took an army of people to turn you into the person you are today.

CHAPTER 8

LIVE A LIFE OF SERVICE

"The best way to find yourself is to lose yourself in the service of others."

—Mahatma Gandhi

One family. Two sons. Two different paths toward greatness.

From the first son, Scooter, we learned about how to assemble a winning team. But it was from the second son, Adam, that I learned one of the most important lessons of all.

I met Adam Braun at a Summit Series conference called Summit at Sea, a kind of summer camp for people who want to change the world. When you see Adam for the first time, he seems like just a regular person, not a superhuman athlete or high-rolling entrepreneur like some of the others you've met in this book. He doesn't have the rock star, Hollywood swagger of his brother. He has an Ivy League pedigree, but I don't think anyone would consider him to be an intimidating genius. He's a regular guy with a big heart, whose high-paying job at a major consulting firm left him dissatisfied and unfulfilled. Like Adam, I, too, had made a little money and had what most people would see as the trappings of success. And as I felt after becoming an All-American in the decathlon, he, too, felt he needed to find some greater purpose, some cause or path to follow.

I could deeply relate to his story that day we met, not just the dissatisfaction but also what it was like to have the shadow of a great sibling follow you and shade your decisions. Given how important my own brother has been to my life, it isn't surprising that I have found myself including brothers as champions of these two chapters. So I consider it serendipity that I encountered Adam—at a conference on a boat, no less—embodying the bold decision to make his life all about giving back.

Adam is the founder of Pencils of Promise, a nonprofit group that has built more than 300 schools and changed the lives of hundreds of thousands of children around the world. Actually, wait, he wouldn't like that I said *nonprofit*. He prefers the term *for purpose.* That purpose is helping kids learn and follow their dreams—kids that most of us pretend don't exist. More recently, his *New York Times* best-selling book, *The Promise of a Pencil,* has brought Adam into a much brighter spotlight, but for the past several years he has been building one of the most important charitable education organizations in the world.

There were two seminal events in Adam's life that set him on his unique path. The first occurred when he was

17 years old and a promising basketball player on an AAU team. His parents made the decision to take in two young athletes from Mozambique named Sam and Cornelio. Not unlike what Leigh Anne and Sean Tuohy did for Michael Oher in a story made famous by Michael Lewis in his book *The Blind Side,* Adam's parents wanted to give these kids a chance to fulfill their potential and experience the American dream. For Adam, his parents' choice was a chance to expand his definition of family by adding two incredible people to it.

Sam was a senior when he came to live with the Braun family. He stayed through his senior year, graduated, then went to Brown University. Cornelio was a sophomore and lived in their house for 3 years before getting a full ride to Georgetown and then transferring to American University after freshman year, from where he ultimately graduated. To this day, Adam considers Sam and Cornelio his brothers. One lives in Los Angeles, the other in DC, and they celebrate all their family events together. Their kids are Adam's nieces and nephews.

"Not only did it change the dynamic of our family, but also it entirely changed my personal worldview. I started to realize the path that Sam and Cornelio had taken was the path that people had taken over generations who wanted to strive for a life that was more than the one that they were born into. It opened my eyes up to how many cultures and people exist outside of that small bubble that I had experienced until that point growing up in Fairfield County, Connecticut, really only seeing New England," he told me.

AN UNLIKELY JOURNEY

This was the first step in Adam's path toward greatness. A step that led to aspirations for living a very different life than most people would consider the norm. As a sophomore at Brown University, inspired by his family experience and the powerful 1992 documentary *Baraka*, Adam enrolled to attend Semester at Sea (noticing a boat theme here?), an academic program aboard a large cruise ship that hosts students from all around the country while circumnavigating the globe and visiting numerous countries over the course of about 100 days. Adam had a friend who had been on Semester at Sea, and upon her return, she could not stop raving about her experience. Their stop in India was particularly transformative for her, which in turn was transformative for him, because it just so happened to be a scene in *Baraka* shot in Varanasi, India, that had enthralled Adam with all the potential the world held outside his bubble.

"So I looked at the Semester at Sea itinerary, and they were going to India. I thought, 'This is it. I'm going to go to India, go to Varanasi, and also get to see all these other incredible places around the world,'" Adam told me. As he spoke, I could hear the purpose in his voice. "Sometimes you just have this inner voice that compels you. It's your future self speaking to your present self, saying, 'Follow me. This is who and what you were meant to be.'"

For a moment, however, it appeared that Adam was meant to be at the bottom of the Pacific Ocean. Eight hundred miles offshore, shortly after leaving port, the Semester at Sea ship was hit by a 60-foot rogue wave that could have easily sunk the boat and taken everyone on board with it. His journey around the world nearly ended before it began. This near-death experience put Adam in a particularly vulnerable and introspective place as they continued their travels from country to country. Here they would come, week after week, working with, meeting, and learning from all these people who didn't have much; yet in nearly every case, they were met with unexpected levels of happiness that, to Adam, seemed so scant in the materialistic culture he'd left just months ago.

I imagine that this is what led to the conversation that completely changed Adam's life: "Everyone on Semester at Sea did this thing where they collect one thing per country—a beer bottle or a funny hat, or they got a T-shirt, or they took a photo of a Beanie Baby in front of a landmark. My thing was asking one kid per country what they would want if they could have anything in the world."

When Adam started telling me this story, the implications for my own life hit me right away. For a college kid to have that kind of awareness of others, that kind of empathy, was inspiring. For all my focus and perseverance and hustle when I was playing sports in high school and college, I was also pretty selfish and egotistical. I thought mostly about myself instead of how I could help the other guys around me, and when I look back on it, I'm pretty sure that held me back from achieving the kind of happiness and success I was looking for. As selfless as Adam's "one thing" was, his worldview was still dominated by his life inside the Connecticut bubble, and he wanted to escape it.

"I expected to get answers from these kids that were similar to what I wanted when I was a kid, which was, like, a big house, a fancy car, and the latest technology," Adam admitted. "But the answers were just so different."

The most powerful one came from a little boy begging on the outskirts of the city of Agra in northern India. Adam asked him, "If you could have anything in the world, what would it be?" His answer was simple: "I want a pencil." That's it. Just a stick of wood with some graphite in it. As you can imagine, he probably wasn't too particular about whether it was a number 2 Dixon Ticonderoga pencil or a fancy mechanical one, he was willing to take anything. Why? This precious little boy wanted to *learn,* to go to school, and he believed the pencil was the thing that would get him there.

Even hearing this conversation gives me inspired chills. I know what you're thinking. It shook Adam to his core, motivated him to give up all his worldly possessions and dedicate himself to changing the world, right? Wrong. It did indeed leave an indelible mark on the young man—but he had a bigger vision than becoming a martyr.

MAKING THE VISION A REALITY

After his semester wrapped up, Adam headed back to America, where he did what many in his position would do: get a job in corporate America where he made tons of money. Seriously. It's almost become a cliché to complain about how students from elite universities head to Wall Street, but that's exactly what Adam did.

He found himself with a job offer from Bain, one of the world's most successful (and some say ruthless) consulting firms. And when you hear Adam's explanation of what he learned, you understand why he made this seemingly superficial decision: "I went to work at Bain & Company on the consulting side and just went through this incredible training work with absolutely brilliant people, saw the inner workings of Fortune 500 companies, had exposure to how the best businesses in the world were run and even improved upon."

Are you seeing now? Yes, that moment in the street in India changed Adam, but he knew besides handing the kid a pencil, there was nothing much he could do for him in the way of real change. Adam went to work in corporate America precisely to learn the skills, build the relationships, and earn the money he needed to effect the change he wanted to see. In other words, unlike so many young people who find themselves with good jobs at places with names like Goldman Sachs, Google, and BP, Adam wasn't doing it for himself or for the money.

"I realized about a year, year and a half in, two things. The first was that the nonprofits I was passionate about weren't run with any of the business acumen that I was used to seeing." There's no question most nonprofits have their hearts in the right place, but according to Adam: "When you're actually inside of the organizations, they're incredibly inefficient. It's because they're usually based on passion. So the language that I spoke, the sense that I had around business, it was kind of weird and frustrating to me that these humanitarian issues weren't being approached with the same commitment to results."

There was another benefit from being around sharks in suits. He realized he didn't want to be one, not for very long anyway. "I got really bored of meeting people at a

bar and them asking, 'What do you do?' and my answer
being, 'Well, I'm a 23-year-old management consultant.'
That's a really boring conversation after about the fifth
time. In a year and a half of living in New York as a young,
20-something single male, I was living what I thought
was this great life. I had this sick apartment and access to
awesome parties and dating different girls and had great
friends around, but I wasn't connected to anything that
wasn't in service of myself."

That's when it hit him: "I didn't want to be a management consultant. I wanted to be somebody who builds
something—specifically, schools internationally for
children in rural communities. That's who I wanted to
become." But now he had the skills and support to be
able to do it.

Bain allows their employees to take what they call
"social impact externships" that offer hands-on experience working on important educational and development
problems out in the world for 6 to 9 months. Essentially,
if you make it through the first 2 years of employment at
the firm (what amounts to a probationary training
period) and they promote you on to a third year, in that
third year they let you leave and follow your passion. You
don't get paid, at least not by Bain, but you can work for
any approved program or company that will bring you on
(and potentially pay you). Adam decided he would do one
of these externships. Initially, he thought he might work
with an organization called the Cambodian Children's
Fund that he had been volunteering for since college as
a fund-raising coordinator selling T-shirts, throwing

parties, and doing pretty much anything that might help
these kids.

Then one night shortly thereafter, he went to the New
York Philharmonic for the first time. "I'd never been to a
symphony before, and this guy walks out onstage to play
a piano concerto and just starts crushing these keys. He
was exuding so much passion into this instrument. I was
just mesmerized by it."

Not only was Adam mesmerized, he was inspired.
The same way that pianist felt about his music, Adam
wanted to feel about . . . anything, really. "I just wanted to
feel that passion, I wanted to feel alive the way that he
must when he connected to that piano. And in that
moment is when this name literally just popped into my
head: Pencils of Promise. It was the perfect name."

It was sort of his Jerry Maguire moment. "I went
home, wrote everything that I could on paper—like an
original mission statement, a charter, a manifesto, all
these stupid fund-raising ideas, all the people I would
contact wherever I would travel who I thought could help
me try to build the school, the very first one. I was really
committed to building the first school and dedicating it
to my grandmother, who was turning 80 that year. She is
a Holocaust survivor and has just been through so much
so that I could be in the position I was in."

He thought, "Let me live in service of her, in particular, honoring her, carrying forward her legacy, and then
ultimately educating children in poverty who don't have
access to high-quality education."

A few weeks later, he went to the bank to open an

account. He asked the teller what the minimum amount required was—the answer was $25. And with that, he launched Pencils of Promise with a $25 check and never looked back.

THE RIGHT KIND OF ROI

The organization he built meshed Adam's for-profit business acumen with his nonprofit idealism, a model that attracted me. For a few years prior to meeting Adam, I knew I wanted to start giving back and serving others outside of my business, but I didn't know how or what to do. After meeting Adam, I decided this was something I could get behind because even though I never felt like I was a smart kid growing up, I was drawn to learning, I yearned for knowledge, and I valued every type of education on my path to success. I got involved with Adam's organization and donated money to build a school in Guatemala.

Part of the mission of Pencils of Promise is to have the local community take ownership of their school. To do that, the community must build the school themselves. The organization supplies the materials and a contractor with know-how, but the mothers and fathers build the school. The result is an enormous level of pride and stewardship. Investing their own sweat equity, they are determined to keep the school maintained and functioning. I love this mission and follow these principles in my own business with my students. I provide the content, oversight, materials, and tools necessary through my podcast, products, and services, but I don't "do the work for them."

If I did, I'd be enabling them instead of empowering them to use their own genius and talents to learn the skills by executing. This way, they can reap the rewards and have much more ownership and pride in what they create.

Talking to Adam is uplifting and inspiring. "As much as I'm a passion-driven person, my background helped immensely because I'm now an entrepreneur who filters every decision through the question 'Will this provide long-term ROI?'" he said. "I always wanted to build an organization with the head of a great business and the heart of a humanitarian idealist."

Think about that: He's not referring to a return *for him.* He means, how can the organization best be of service and deliver the most value to the people it's meant to serve?

I heard a similar sentiment from Angel about his philosophy as a CEO at Deckers: "Greatness to me is just about being there for other people; living a life that is others oriented is where you achieve greatness." That's how Angel tries to think and act as a leader of more than 2,300 employees with their own stories, dreams, hopes, and needs. "Deckers is about all the people who work here having the kind of opportunity that I had, to live a life that maybe is outside of your expectations or your practical reality or that you dream about but don't have the vehicle. I say, 'Here is the vehicle.'"

That's what a true leader, a really great individual, does, whether they run a for-profit or a for-purpose organization. It's not all about you; it's not all about what you want and need. If you want to achieve those things, I've learned, you have to actively and regularly help other people with their own wants and needs. Only then, when you've moved away from selfishness, can your winning team truly thrive.

In our self-centered world, it's easy to buy into the "me" mentality. We are constantly told that to get ahead, we need to invest in ourselves, and then once we've "made it," we can give back. But as Adam Braun's story shows, giving back can be the vehicle to "making it" if we align our service with our passion. Without service, achievement is empty.

A LONGER, RICHER LIFE

James Clear, the entrepreneur and travel photographer, wrote about this on his blog after reading a 2012 *New York Times* article about the research on longevity:

> The article didn't come out and say it, but what it alluded to was that as people age, they tend to find themselves consuming more and creating less. To put it bluntly: The easiest way to live a short unimportant life is to consume the world around you rather than contribute to it.
>
> Meanwhile, the people who keep on contributing tend to be the ones who keep on living. The message was clear. People who contribute to their community live longer.

If greatness isn't a good enough reason to be of service to others, I think James has given you the biggest reason of all—a longer life. Still, I get why you might be hesitant. *Service* is such a loaded term. Fortunately, being of service also has many definitions and iterations. It doesn't mean you have to work in a soup kitchen or take a vow of poverty or work for a nonprofit.

One of my favorite TED talks is by a guy named Ron Finley, who is known as the "guerilla gardener." For years, he has been planting vegetable gardens across South Central Los Angeles. Why? For fun, for the beauty, for food, and to make a small contribution to a neighborhood that desperately needs it. I love this because he isn't asking for anything in return, nor does he expect someone to pay for these services. He simply does this as a random act of kindness to give back and make his community that much more colorful and fruitful. He takes pride in his community and adds his gifts to it. It makes me think about creative ways I can add to my community as well.

Kyle Maynard is of service to veterans—even though he isn't one himself and his injuries were biological instead of the result of violence. But by connecting with these service members, by seeking out challenges and bigger goals, he provides an inspirational service.

Shawn Johnson speaks on behalf of the Women's Sports Foundation, which was founded by tennis legend Billie Jean King back in 1974 to boost the lives of girls through sports and physical activity. Shawn's taking everything she learned from her Olympic and dancing success and paying it forward to a generation of young girls who might need the same kind of boost that the little boy in India needed from Adam Braun.

The other side of my buddy Aubrey Marcus, the CEO of Onnit who gave us the exercise on what's MISSING in Chapter 5, is essentially one giant quest to serve humanity by exploring the possibilities of human happiness and consciousness. He wants everyone to transcend everything, and he works exhaustingly and selflessly to that end—through his dedication to researching the optimal ways for total human optimization using the success of his fitness and nutrition business to make it possible.

I get the sense from many of the authors whom I've learned so much from that they would have written their books for free if they had to. They not only felt that some sort of muse had struck them and they owed it to their art to get it out, but they genuinely felt the world needed to hear their message and would be better if they read it.

I don't think traditional charity is the only way to act with purpose or be in service of others. Every day, I wake up and feel excited about my podcast not because of the important people *I* get to meet but, rather, because I get to serve as a conduit between them and my audience. I get to learn and help others learn, too. That thought has also helped power me through this book.

That's my point: You can be of service by following your passion. As Adam Smith wrote, "It is not from the benevolence of the butcher, the brewer, or the baker that we expect our dinner, but from their regard to their own interest." Following your passion instead of settling, subsuming yourself as part of a larger goal—that is the first step in being of service to others. But I hope you won't stop there. I hope you'll also see how you can apply your gifts to a big cause and give back without any strings.

Like many successful people, I receive requests for lunch meetings or get asked for advice by people just starting out. They want free coaching, introductions, or a perusal of their business plan. I'm busy, my time is valuable, and the temptation is to say, "Look, I'm sorry, but I don't have the time." And who would fault someone for declining a request for free help? The answer to that question is *you*. You and I, if we are to be great, need to practice empathy and help others. We need to think: "I was once in this person's shoes, and someone helped me out." Like Kyle and Shawn and Aubrey and Angel, we should always be paying it forward.

I'm not saying you need to give an hour of your time to everyone who asks for advice, as you may never get anything done in your own life if you are that popular! However, maybe this means taking a few extra minutes to help a new coworker. Maybe it's pointing out something you noticed in a competitor's game that would help them improve. Maybe it's speaking at your kid's career day. Maybe it's writing an article about a sensitive topic that most people are too ashamed to share their experiences about. Maybe it's smiling at a stranger on the street or helping them pick up something they dropped. For me, it was starting *The School of Greatness* podcast so I could help all those people I couldn't reach or carve out the time for.

It took me a long time to understand how crucial a life of service is to achieving greatness in any discipline. Adam Braun clearly got this early on and parlayed that insight into an amazing career as a social entrepreneur.

Nelson Mandela put it best when he said, "There is no passion to be found playing small and settling for a life that is less than the one you are capable of living."

But Adam realized that thinking about yourself, your bank account, or whatever it happens to be is thinking small. As he puts it, "My definition of greatness would be living a life full of purpose, love, and dignity."

I'll add to that: *for yourself and for others.* I know what you're capable of. I know you can be of service in so many ways.

EXERCISE #1:
Choose Your Avenue of Service

Get involved in giving back, whether it is through your time, talent, or treasure (dollars).

Step 1

Write down something simple you can do *today* to give back to your community, family, and friends or a stranger. Your service can start as a random act of kindness. You could open a door for someone, buy flowers for a stranger, give a compliment, fill someone's expired parking meter, help someone in need, or simply smile. Give back in some way with a positive purpose. You will immediately experience the intrinsic reward whether the act is seen or unseen.

Doing this on a consistent basis, you will quickly find

yourself living a life in service to others that does not feel like it is taking away from some other part of your life. Instead, it will feel additive and necessary—like eating or breathing. As your daily acts of kindness grow, you can research a charity, a nonprofit, or an organization you would like to get involved with. Here is some food for thought.

- Education in your community
- The arts (dance, music, theater)
- Advocating for human rights
- Mentorship programs
- Cancer research
- Fund-raising

The possibilities are endless. Whatever you are inspired by and speaks to you, that is exactly what you should be doing. If an organization is not working for you, start your own! Anything is possible, so get involved and spread the word. There are tons of opportunities out there. Stop thinking about what people will say or how they will look at you and be proud to take a stand for the service you have chosen.

For specific organizations that I believe in and more suggestions, check out schoolofgreatness.com/resources.

Step 2

After deciding on your avenue of service, identify how you can best serve it through your time, talent, or treasure.

Time

Some of us have more time to give and can volunteer directly. Offer your time to volunteer with the organization of your choice. Be consistent, whether it's weekly, monthly, or yearly, in order to create a positive habit.

Talent

You might have a certain talent that organizations need (maybe you're great at graphic design, and an organization needs help with their logo or Web site development). Reach out to these organizations to offer your expertise. Many organizations have a tremendous vision and all the hustle in the world, but they struggle finding a great team. You can be the difference.

Treasure

If you do not feel like you have the time or talent to give directly to an organization, financial donations impact growing organizations disproportionately. Sending $1,000 to the Red Cross is great, but giving $500 to your local veterans group or pediatric cancer charity can change their month. This month, commit to a monthly donation to a campaign or a cause.

Now make a decision about how you intend to get involved and write it down. Make it real. One or all of the three Ts? Then choose a date that you are going to begin and prepare to take action!

EXERCISE #2:
Do Your First Act

Short and sweet, you've got to put your money (or time or talent) where your mouth is. This month, go do something with and for your organization of choice. This can be actually volunteering at an event, organizing your own event/fund-raiser, or donating money or goods. As in exercise #1, start small with simple daily acts of kindness and build upon them.

Not only will this get you serious about helping, but you'll also get to feel that amazing high of doing good. Of course, this is worth sharing, so once you've committed to your act, post to your social media channels with a photo and an update to let everyone know what you are doing and how it went (#greatnessbook). This is a great way to encourage and inspire others to get involved. The only thing more contagious than giving is the joy and the emotion that come with it!

COACHING TIP

When you fully understand why giving is the key to life, then you make it part of your daily mission to serve others in whatever you do. Don't look at this as an extra task you need to take on. If you do that, you've missed the point entirely. Rather, look at this as a part of who you are, who you become, and your way of being in every moment.

It needs to be in your breath, rushing through your blood. Every aspect of your life should have a component of service. It can be as small as smiling at everyone you come across to as big and broad as you want to take it. There is no right or wrong level of giving; the key is just that you give from a place of love instead of guilt. The way I am sure to do that is a little trick I developed after flying all over the country speaking to and meeting with people just like you. I remind myself of that part of the preflight safety announcement that every flight attendant gives:

Put your own mask on first.

When you make sure your needs are met and you are full, then you'll have even more energy to give to others. Go out and live a life of service!

CONCLUSION

In 2012, I moved from New York to Los Angeles for a girl, arriving with two big bags, a guitar, and a smile on my face. Later that night, she broke up with me. What made it worse was that my life in New York was on fire before leaving for LA! My business was thriving, my relationships were growing, I was doing cool stuff all the time. I felt invincible. This move out to LA for love was just one more thing I was going to conquer. Instead, it put me right on my ass.

We were in our mid- and late twenties at the time, so of course our breakup wasn't actually final. We got back together, dating off and on for a few months. I committed to being the perfect boyfriend, doing everything I could do to make my girlfriend happy and our relationship healthy, but I knew it wasn't right, it wasn't working. Everything about LA wasn't working, really. I was in a bad head space. Everything that was happening left me frustrated, confused, and uncertain about the future. I would soon learn that, as my friend Kyle Maynard says: We are only as good and as strong as our adversity makes us. Sometimes we don't know what is working against us until we make our biggest mistakes, and I was about to discover that on the journey to greatness, you sometimes have to fall.

One afternoon I was playing pickup basketball at the courts down the street from my condo building when everything came to a head. I had been guarding this one guy all game—he was a little older than I was and definitely a little heavier—and he had been talking trash and throwing dirty elbows the entire time. Now, I'm a relentless competitor and have been in all areas of my life for as long as I can remember. I can take some trash talk and some hard fouls in the spirit of competition. But this guy was starting to get personal, and he was trying to assert himself over me—dominating me, like an alpha dog.

What he didn't know—and neither did I, really—was that this behavior was one of my major triggers. Being disrespected and dehumanized made me see red. We got in each other's faces. There was a lot of shouting and posturing, literally puffing out and beating our chests like a couple of gorillas trying to show dominance. I was beside myself with anger. I couldn't understand why he was doing this to me. Then he took it a step further and head-butted me right in the face. This was no warning love tap, like you see sometimes in NBA games when two alpha dogs square up against each other after a hard foul around the basket. I couldn't believe how hard he slammed his forehead into mine!

If you've never been head-butted, let me tell you, it *hurts!* It makes you see stars, and it makes your eyes water. And if you're me, it makes you lose your mind a little. I am not proud of what I did next. I pounded on the guy with every ounce of energy I could muster. Eventually, my best friend, Matt, whom I was playing with, grabbed the guy, and his teammate pulled me off to break us up. Unfortunately, it didn't end there. The guy was still talking trash and insulting me, and I was screaming at him, asking why he would do that to me. Why would he head-butt me like that? What was he thinking? Why did he attack me over a meaningless pickup basketball game?

The questions were rhetorical, mostly. I was basically talking to myself, trying to process what the hell was going on. But this guy decided to answer. I don't remember what he said—it was all kind of a blur—but whatever it was, I responded by running up to him and hitting him one last time as hard as I could.

It was one of those moments like out of a movie. The basketball court went dead quiet except for the sound of my yelling and screaming. I was yelling at everyone, telling them that he hit me first, and I was screaming at him for attacking me. I still couldn't understand it. My friend Matt told me I should get out of there before anything else happened, so I ran. No, I *sprinted* the blocks back to my building, bounded up 11 flights of stairs, burst through my apartment door into my bedroom, and collapsed onto my bed shaking uncontrollably. What the hell just happened? I felt completely out of control and completely terrified of my own behavior.

That's not me. I'm not a fighter. I aspire to come from a place of total love. Why did I react like that?

I repeated those words to myself over and over in my head. The feelings I was being forced to wrestle with were almost totally foreign. I hadn't felt like this in nearly 20 years—since the last time I got into a similar fight as a kid. Lying on my bed looking up at the ceiling, I started thinking about that earlier fight. What I realized very quickly was that this fight was practically a carbon copy of that one.

It happened when I was 12 years old, back in Ohio. Three of us were raking leaves and grass along a path on the golf course where we worked during the summer. Two of us were goofing around and roughhousing. We were playing this game where we'd rake up a little bit of grass, then flip the rake over and flick the grass and leaves at the other person, almost like you'd pick up and throw a lacrosse ball. It was a fun little grass fight. We decided to bring the other kid into the fun. He was older than we were (15), so we decided we couldn't ask him—that probably wouldn't be cool—we would just have to tag-team him a little. The two of us scooped up some grass and leaves at the same time and flicked it at him simultaneously.

At the time, we cracked up, thinking he would join in and playfully fight back. We were half right. As we turned back to keep grass-fighting each other, the 15-year-old kid came up behind me and punched me in the back of the head. I was stunned. Then I was confused. Then I was stark raving furious. All within the span of 2 seconds, I whipped around and hit the kid square across the face with my rake handle. The blow sent him to the ground, and I pounced him. I hit him with everything I had, screaming at him the whole time like in that scene from *A Christmas Story* when Ralphie finally snaps and beats the snot out of Scut Farkus.

Finally, the other kid got behind me and pulled me off in a full nelson. I shook free and sprinted the 500 yards to the clubhouse, where I burst through the employee entrance, ran into the bathroom, and started washing my hands. Like if I washed away the evidence and got home before anyone else saw me, it meant it didn't happen. My knuckles were scraped bloody. Dirt and grass and blood poured into the sink and swirled down the drain. When I finished and stopped shaking, I came out into the office and there was the 15-year-old. He was screaming at me, "Why did you do that, Lewis?! What is wrong with you?!" I barely heard him, because I was sick to my stomach about what had just happened. Seeing what I was capable of when I let my emotions get the best of me, I vowed right then and there to never fight again.

I succeeded in upholding that vow . . . for 17 years. Lying on my bed staring up at the ceiling, a 29-year-old man with bruised and bloodied knuckles, connecting the dots between those two moments and seeing the parallels, scared me to death. I had to do something about this. I had to figure out what was going on inside of me and why. What had happened to me? And most important, why did I allow this to happen?

Two months later, at the suggestion of my friend Quddus, who'd heard about the fight and the troubles I was having, I signed up for Chris Lee's leadership workshop. Little did I know, being an effective leader requires emotional intelligence, and that's a lot of what we covered. We talked about triggers and being open and vulnerable. All the stuff we discussed in Chapter 3: Cultivate a Champion's Mindset. Why did being attacked unfairly like that turn me into the Hulk? Why was perceived disrespect or feeling taken advantage of such a trigger for me?

Chris helped me trace these emotions back through my life, teaching me how to be vulnerable and open to my past. And that's when it clicked. It all went back to the time when I was 5 years old and I was raped by my babysitter's teenage son. I won't dive into specifics, because that is not what this book is about.* What I will say is that after opening up and sharing this story with

---

*If you want to hear the full story about what I learned about this experience and the good that has come from it, my dear friend Jonathan Fields interviewed me in episode 61 of my podcast.

listeners of my podcast, I was overwhelmed with love
and support from all over the world. I also came to realize just how many people have been affected by sexual
abuse in their lives. Listener after listener e-mailed me
emotional, heartbreaking stories about their childhood
traumas. It pains me to see how many people have experienced their own version of what I went through.**

Before attending this workshop, I had never shared
that story with anyone. I'd kept it locked inside for almost
25 years, trying to forget it, trying to deny that it ever happened. But I couldn't anymore. It had planted these triggers
in my mind that were starting to sabotage every area of my
life—my romantic relationship, my friendships, my business partnerships, my overall confidence and happiness.

With Chris's guidance, I stood up in front of the group
at his leadership workshop and shared the story publicly
for the first time. And it was a revelation. I had been too
scared, too hurt, too superficial to look deep down inside
myself and face my own past until that moment. We all
have traumas. We all have secret pain. We all make mistakes. It's true. I wish it wasn't so, but it is.

That's the bad news. The good news is that we're all
also capable of greatness no matter what we've been
through. In fact, it's our past that makes us who we are
and our adversity has the potential to become our greatest advantage. You see, the breakdown I experienced in
my life which exploded on the basketball court earlier
that year led to a profound and life-changing breakthrough. I didn't know I was holding onto that kind of

---

** If you are a male who has experienced sexual abuse in your life, check out 1in6.org for
more information and guidance. For general support, check out rainn.org.

rage inside nor that I was capable of being so violent. Going back into my memories and becoming aware of the stories I had told myself about the pain I experienced as a child was one of the keys to moving from reacting to responding in my life. I was truly disappointed in myself after that incident, and I committed to discovering what was holding me back from really being the man I said I was and wanted to be. By clearing and coming clean about my past, I was able to align my actions with my values and learn new ways of showing up in the world that were previously counterintuitive: Things like cultivating a win-win environment in everything I do, seeing the power in vulnerability, acknowledging my emotions, and holding myself accountable to my vision every day.

THE SCHOOL OPENS FOR BUSINESS

I began *The School of Greatness* podcast in the months between my big fight on the basketball court and my time with Chris. My first guest was the brilliant *New York Times* best-selling author of *The 48 Laws of Power*, Robert Greene, and we were going to talk about his (then) new book, *Mastery*. Just being in Robert's presence, this man who had not only written several classic, timeless books but had influenced multiplatinum rappers, fashion designers, and world leaders, was inspiring.

As we sat and talked, Robert spoke about how much time and energy and effort it takes to become truly skilled at something. It had taken him decades to get to where he was, and it had taken the greats of history he wrote about just as long, if not longer. He talked about the critical importance of apprenticeship and studying under other masters. That's where I got the idea to craft my own curriculum, to enroll in a new kind of school where I could learn and reach my potential. The title of that first episode with Robert on my newly launched podcast, *The School of Greatness,* was "How to Master Anything and Achieve Greatness." I wanted to do both those things very badly.

Like anything new on the Internet, the podcast had its ups and downs at first. I was learning as I went, trying new things, figuring out most of it all by myself. I had no idea what I was doing. But I also didn't know what I didn't know, so anything was possible. Shortly after Chris's workshop, *The School of Greatness* podcast began to take on a new life and renewed energy. Regular listeners noticed a huge change in the way I connected with guests, how open I was, and how my ego had shifted. I'd learned so much from Chris—and the lessons I learned about myself from his workshop had quite literally changed my life.

The goal now was not just to learn from great, interesting people but to finally get serious about the goals and vision I had for myself as a young man. Yes, I'd accomplished some things in life, but I wasn't fully happy. I knew I could do more. I knew I wanted more. So I availed myself of some of the greatest minds, thinkers, and doers in the world. I put myself at their feet and learned everything I could.

The chapters you've just read are the essence of that education. They are my lecture notes, filtered through the experiences and struggles I've gone through in trying to integrate them into my life.

From Angel Martinez I learned the power and importance of creating a clear vision. He taught me that *you become what you envision yourself being.* I will never forget those words.

From Kyle Maynard and Nicole Lapin I learned that there is no room in our lives for excuses, especially if greatness is our goal. Greatness is what happens when your talent and your vision face adversity, and you persist in the face of it to learn the language of the new, the scary, and the unfamiliar.

From Shawn Johnson I learned that greatness is not about making it to the top of the medal stand. It is a mindset that is fundamentally about belief in yourself and your ability to accomplish your goals.

From my brother, Christian, I learned that there is no shame in hustle. If you want to be great, you have to work harder and smarter. When something knocks you down—when someone says no—you have to be able to pick yourself up, dust yourself off, and do it all over again.

From Rich Roll, Chalene Johnson, Aubrey Marcus, and Shawn Stevenson to many other wellness masters I've studied with, I learned the importance of physical health to greatness, no matter what the dream or the vision. You have a choice—to move, to eat well, to sleep right—and that choice, if you don't make it soon enough and completely enough, *will* stand in your way on the path to greatness, no matter what else you bring to the table.

From my old buddy Graham Holmberg I learned that it's never too late or too insignificant to develop and practice positive habits, no matter how naturally talented you might be. Those habits are the backbone of the routine that will inch you closer every day to greatness.

From Scooter Braun I learned the critical role of building and leading a winning team to the pursuit of any kind of great achievement. Strong relationships with great people who have positive energy are fundamental to that team.

From Adam Braun, I learned the power of being in service to others. I learned that you don't have to wait until you make it to serve the world. In fact, being of service, in any number of different ways, can be the path to making it.

And now that we're near the end of the book, I have another thing to say: This isn't the end of the road. This isn't a typical school. There is no graduation ceremony. There is no cessation of classes or summer break. The School of Greatness is sort of like the Hotel California: You can check out anytime you like, but you can never leave. What I mean is, these lessons will stay with you always—and their application should never end.

I also mean this in the sense that you can't get kicked out either. Lord knows I should have been expelled, banned, or written off for my inexcusable violence. Or I should have been placed on academic probation for the times I slacked off and reverted to old bad habits— despite my professors' having taught me better. But that's not how this works. That's not how *life* works.

Greatness is a voluntary degree. Its study is self-administered. That means *it's all on you.* And you get out of life what you put into it. I hope you pursue it with everything you've got. I hope we bump into each other learning from the same master. Actually, I hope one day I might even take a course from you, and you a course from me.

We're in this together. It's time to go out there and do something great!

ACKNOWLEDGMENTS

Thank you to my family. I'm so blessed to have you all in my life and constantly learn from you as your youngest brother and child. To my father, Ralph, who taught me that time was an illusion and that my age and experience level didn't matter in my pursuit of greatness. You supported all of my dreams, taught me they were always possible, and helped me do whatever it took to make them a reality. You are the best dad I could have ever asked for, and I'm so grateful to be your son. To my mother, Diana, I'm the luckiest child in the world, and you've always supported my crazy ideas, even when they scared you. Thanks for letting me finally play football at 15, even when you were scared I would get hurt. I did get some bruises, but I had years of fun and learned many lessons that made me who I am today. To Chris, you are my hero and the brother I've always looked up to. Your hustle taught me how to be the driven human I am now. To Heidi, my spiritual protector and voice of reason, thank you for opening my heart and guiding me toward love. To Katherine, without your support while living on your couch for over a year (rent free), none of this would have been possible. You are the definition of unconditional love.

To every teacher, house parent, and coach I had during my experience at Principia schools, thank you for giving me structure and guidance I needed the most during that time. You exemplified living a life of service. To Brian Morse, Tom Bania, and Ann Pierson—thank you!

Seven years prior to publishing this book, I read the book *The 4-Hour Workweek* by Tim Ferriss that influenced me to start my journey. Thank you, Tim, for opening my mind to what is possible so I could create the life of my dreams.

To my agent, Stephen Hanselman, thanks for believing in me. You supported my vision to write the book that I've always wanted to publish. Your guidance has been legendary, and this book wouldn't be this great without you. Thanks to Glenn Rifkin for guiding me in the initial development, structure, and layout of this book.

A huge thanks to Ryan Holiday and Nils Parker at Brass Check for writing this book with me and advising on the message and positioning along the way.

And to Heidi Howes and my entire team for helping with the editing to take the book across the finish line. I appreciate and am grateful for all of you!

To Marisa Vigilante, Mary Ann Naples, Gail Gonzales, Yelena Nesbit, Aly Mostel (along with Amy Stanton and team), and the entire family at Rodale, along with Jeffrey Capshew, Melissa Miceli, Holly Smith, Elena Guzman, Nora Flaherty, Patti Hughes, Eve Fitzgerald, and the rest of the powerful army! Thanks for your countless hours and support in getting this out to the world!

To my three main mentors, Stuart Jenkins, Frank Agin, and Chris Hawker, who believed in me when I was broke and broken and had nothing but a dream, you all stepped up when I needed support the most early on. I'll always be grateful for your level of service and for giving so much to me when I could do nothing for you at the time.

To my team that supported me for countless hours during the writing of this book, Matt Cesaratto, Sarah Livingstone, Brittany Rice, Christine Baird, Aja Wiltshire, and Diana Howes—thank you! We are making a powerful impact together!

To Ian Robinson, thank you for guiding me early on with my podcast editing, and to Pat Flynn, Derek Halpern, Ramit Sethi, James Wedmore, and John Lee Dumas, thank you for the inspiration to launch it.

To everyone who has been on *The School of Greatness* podcast, this wouldn't be possible without your incredible wisdom and lessons that you shared with all of us!

Robert Greene, Bob Harper, Tim Ferriss, Bryan Clay, Graham Holmberg, David Anderson, Grant Cardone, Drew Canole, Rich Roll, Jamie Eason, Alex Day, Lissa Rankin, John Romaniello, Adam Bornstein, Adam Grant, Ben Nemtin, Don Yaeger, Kyle Maynard, James Altucher, Pat Flynn, Shawn Johnson, Jon Acuff, Jeff Spencer, Quddus Philippe, Carl Paoli, Leyla Naghizada, Tony Blauer, Ameer Rosic, Chris Hawker, Travis Brewer, Mignon Fogarty, Nick Onken, Aubrey Marcus, Chris Lee, AJ Jacobs, Marc Ecko, Derek Halpern, Danielle LaPorte, Gary Vaynerchuk, Guy Winch, Daniel Negreanu, Sean Stephenson, Christian Howes, Adam In-Q, Josh Shipp, Simon Sinek, Marc Fitt, Charlie Hoehn, Steven Kotler, Liz Wolfe, Adam Braun, Alison Levine, Chris Ducker, Simone de la Rue, Glennon Melton, Jennifer Paige, Alexis Carra, Ryan Holiday, Bryan Bishop, Noah Kagan, John Jantsch, Joe De Sena, Timothy Sykes,

Carmine Gallo, Chris Bailey, Jason SurfrApp, Jordan
Harbinger, CJ Baran, Ramit Sethi, Bo Eason, Tucker
Max, Branden Hampton, Brendan Schaub, AJ Roberts,
Brett McKay, Scott Barry Kaufman, Jim Afremow,
Chris Guillebeau, Hunter McIntyre, Chalene Johnson,
Dave Asprey, Mike Michalowicz, Tim Larkin, Christine
Hassler, Dan Schawbel, Kevin Kelly, Krista Tippett, DJ Irie,
Kelly Starrett, Tim Ryan, Daniel Amen, Vanessa Van
Edwards, Bill Harris, Ryan Blair, Jairek Robbins, Tony
Robbins, Robbie Rogers, Michael Hyatt, Rory Vaden,
Jim Kwik, Yuri Elkaim, Scott Harrison, Keith Ferrazzi,
Baratunde Thurston, Eric Thomas, Shawn Stevenson,
Angel Martinez, Michele Promaulayko, Scooter Braun,
Nicole Lapin, Donald Schultz, Mikkel Svane, Vani Hari,
Marie Forleo, Peter Bregman, Marc Goodman, Jack Canfield,
David Allen, Kabir Sehgal, Julianne Hough, AJ Hawk,
Todd Kashdan, Amanda Enayati, Eric Greitens, Abel James,
Jeff Goins, Than Merrill, Dorie Clark, Lee Cockerell,
Dale Partridge, Amy Wilkinson, Rob Bell, Jay Papasan,
Cassey Ho, Sally Hogshead, Arianna Huffington, Kristina
Carrillo-Bucaram, Bill Phillips, Jeff Krasno, Gretchen
Rubin, Matthew Hussey, Darren Hardy, Kimberly Guilfoyle,
Dan Millman, Donovan Green, Suzy Welch, Justine Ezarik,
Jacob Lief, Tom Bilyeu, Prince Ea, Nick Symmonds, Rick
Hanson, Laird Hamilton, Gabrielle Reece, Jackie Warner,
Fabio Viviani, Bryan Johnson, and the future guests that
will inspire the world!

To all my friends and supporters, thank you for being
there and inspiring me every step of the way!

INDEX